SCREENWRITING
IS STORYTELLING

SCREENWRITING IS STORYTELLING

Creating an A-List Screenplay That Sells!

KATE WRIGHT

Foreword by Arthur Hiller

A PERIGEE BOOK

A Perigee Book
Published by The Berkeley Publishing Group
A division of Penguin Group (USA) Inc.
375 Hudson Street
New York, New York 10014

Perigee trade paperback edition: October 2004

Perigee trade paperback ISBN: 0-399-53024-X

Visit our website at www.penguin.com

This book has been cataloged by the Library of Congress

Printed in the United States of America

10   9   8   7   6   5   4   3   2   1

To the gifted storytellers who taught me,
especially Tennessee, Jason, Robaire, Lenore, and Jim

Acknowledgments

THANKING those who have influenced me and supported me over the years is such a privilege . . .

The capacity to develop a worldview is a gift, but there are those who, by their generosity of spirit, have helped me to shape a perspective that sustains me: my parents, siblings, and extended family, the Jesuits of Georgetown University, the producers of Paulist Productions. Not enough can be attributed to my sister, Marguerite, about whom it could be said that no matter what road you take in life you will always meet her on her way back.

It is said that we create our own opportunities, but there are so many who generously open the doors for us as we move along: U.S. Senator John Culver, Michael Eisner, Patricia Sarcone, Arthur Hiller, Ted Field, Robert Butler, Harry Sherman, Robert Cort, David Madden, Nancy Bein, Marian Brayton, Peter Frankovich, and Kathleen McCarthy.

Dr. Linda Venis, Director of UCLA Extension's Writers Program, and her staff have enthusiastically supported my efforts over the years. By creating a signature class based on this book, I hope to reflect their confidence in me.

The world of the unconscious is a mysterious world, but thanks to Dr. Albert Mason and Dr. Michael Paul, who have guided me with the insight that there is a *truth receptor.* Unconscious experience is unconsciously stored in the human condition: We experience truth even when others don't want us to discover it.

Where would this book be without students who have taught me? A special mention to Carl Kowlessar, Joseph Costa, Chris Koefoed, Doug Mayfield, Lynda Taylor, Dan Brandler, Ethan Wayne, Dawn DeKeyser, Michael Kingston, Reid Denham, Will Tomlinson, Werner Disse, Nancy Smith, Lola Tiegland, Terry Smith, and David Cowper, whose talent and genius have taught me everything you need to know about screenwriting.

There is always someone who jump-starts a project. Dr. Lynda Toth, thank you for recognizing my breadth of experience and introducing me to New York book agent Madeleine Morel, whose dynamic personality shaped the book proposal that quickly landed in the hands of Perigee/Putnam Executive Editor, Sheila Curry Oakes. Sheila's extraordinary skills as an editor continue to amaze and amuse me.

Syd Field, Frank Swertlow, Camilla Broderick, Rochelle Edwards, Theresa Dunn, Colleen Crahan, Heidi Brennan, Judi Fogelman, Lisa Chorna, Judy Hanauer, Guy Levy, Louis Raphael, Paula Navar, and Vanessa Preziose have directly contributed to this book in ways that cannot be measured. My editorial assistant, the ever-curious Athena Schultz, has literally become the point-of-view character within the text—she not only knows the spelling of every actor's name in Hollywood, she requests clarification exactly where it's needed.

Literary agents are the unsung heroes of Hollywood. Martin Shapiro, Michael Shlain, and Dave Warden rule. Rowland Perkins even takes time out for golf.

Lenore Wright and James Carabatsos have been personally generous in every way. They have been my touchstones as storytellers, on the golf course, and in life. Many other talented writers and filmmakers have influenced me to new levels storytelling: David Engelbach, T. S. Cook, Tom Rickman, Michael Nemec, John Riley, John Sacret Young, Frank Pierson, Reginald Rose, Chris Canaan, Chet Walker, Owen Roizman, Robert Butler, James Cameron, Sydney Pollack, Steven Spielberg, Andrew Davis, the late Jason Miller, and the legendary Tennessee Williams.

Love, affection, and friendship sustain us throughout life, especially as we mature. Our loved ones are always with us, even when they're not. God bless the absent ones.

—Kate Wright

CONTENTS

Foreword

STORYTELLING is innate to the human condition. Its underpinnings are cerebral, emotional, communal, psychological. One of the storyteller's main responsibilities is to resonate in the audience's psyche a certain something at the end of it all, to emotionally move the audience, to compel the audience to "get it" on a visceral level.

Screenwriting Is Storytelling holds this responsibility uppermost in mind. How does the writer connect to the "inner story"? How does he or she assure that the audience connects to it as well? Answering these fundamental questions is what distinguishes this book from the scores of how-to books that line library shelves and bookstore displays. It is pitched to a more sophisticated level of thinking about how we, as screenwriters, become storytellers. Aesop may not have been quite as analytical about the process, but, like all good storytellers, knew the "inner story." This book takes the reader to that almost preconscious level of how and why a story resonates with its audience.

Using many popular references as examples, author Kate Wright discusses the theory of storytelling, and then shows how that theory is applied in the commercial world of television and film, demonstrating the complex process by which a writer moves from thinking about an idea, to creating the story concept, to actually writing a major motion picture screenplay.

Unique to this book is the author's approach to the concepts of "spine" and "characterization" as the secret to creating the "magic" in screenwriting. The story's "spine" generates "character behavior" that connects us, as storytellers, to the inner story, and *from inside the story,* we begin to understand what the story is about in a deeper, more meaningful way, as opposed to merely creating the actions of the characters without any dramatic or thematic significance. In the course of creating "spine," a screenwriter must become his or her own characters, and must also assume other personas (psychologist, doctor, engineer, etc.) in order to understand what is happening inside the characters that may be lacking in the story. This book shows how to successfully apply this developmental strategy using *characters as ideas* and *behavior as spine* to create problem-solving story solutions and integrating eight distinctive avenues of thought into the storytelling process.

Emmy Award winner Kate Wright (*Billy, The Conspirator Saint, The Mary Thomas Story,* among others) offers a sophisticated viewpoint distilled from her experience as a film executive, producer, writer, teacher, and script consultant. Her knowledge, wisdom, and experience as a storyteller shine throughout this book, complemented by her vital mind, exquisitely attuned to this complex process of how a writer advances from creating an idea to creating a screenplay. Equally important, she knows how to articulate that mysterious process clearly and concisely.

Kate Wright has enough creative energy to power the sun. Undoubtedly, this book will share a great deal of that light with our modern-day Aesops.

Arthur Hiller, director of *Love Story,*
The In-Laws; former president of the
Directors Guild of America; and
two-term president of The Academy
of Motion Picture Arts and Sciences

Introduction

WORKING with two of America's greatest geniuses, Pulitzer Prize–winning playwright Jason Miller and the legendary Tennessee Williams, offered me a tremendous entrée into the world of storytelling. As major American icons, their extraordinary talent inspired me; and as screenwriters, their remarkable ability to work through the visceral process of storytelling taught me that good stories communicate *simple truths that reflect the poetic dimensions of the human soul.* Now, with twenty years of experience working with geniuses, professionals, associates, and students, I am ready to share my experiences in *Screenwriting Is Storytelling.*

An Emmy Award–winning producer, I have also been a film and television executive, screenwriter, and script consultant. Since 1995, as a UCLA Senior Screenwriting Instructor, I have taught such courses as "Script Doctoring: Rewriting for Productions" and "Writing the Screenplay the Professional Way." Those who work with me tell me consistently that I do not work like anyone else, because I work from inside the story, layer upon layer, emphasizing what the story is about, as opposed to working in linear, plot-emphasizing form. By developing the story on multiple levels before I begin the first draft, I address the *challenge of storytelling,* which opens up the behavioral possibilities within the main character's story throughout the writing of the first draft, into the rewrite, and through the production phase. My experience as a producer has given me the confidence to work this way, and has paid off with projects I have produced or developed with many successful writers, such as Frank Pierson, T. S. Cook, William Hanley, as well as Jason Miller and Tennessee Williams. The best-kept secret about screenwriting, however, comes to those who learn it firsthand by struggling to discover what their story is about *from the inside out.* Although this notion may seem basic, what distinguishes a good screenwriter from a great screenwriter is the humility to recognize that whether we are sitting around a campfire, chatting on a coffee break, or writing a major motion picture screenplay, the task is to tell a story that engages the audience on the most fundamental human level. To do so requires developing the instinct to pinpoint *what the story is* and the willingness to step back as a screenwriter *to discover its depth as a storyteller.* By way of experience, this means screenwriters must become storytellers.

Many of my students have approached screenwriting by rote, attempting to achieve a screenplay by watching movies, taking classes, going to film school, and learning structure. Although this may be a terrific way to become acquainted with the fundamentals of moviemaking, that's not how geniuses like Tennesee Williams or Jason Miller created theatrical masterpieces, and it's not how storytellers like James Cameron, George Lucas, or Sydney Pollack encounter the depth inside their stories that reveal magnificent discoveries about ourselves as human beings.

Storytellers begin by asking "What is my story about?" and continue asking more and more questions until every possible angle of their story is revealed.

In responding to requests from my colleagues, associates, students, and clients to write this book, I began preparing the concept and format by asking them to tell me what they want to learn about screenwriting that they haven't read in a book or discovered on their own. Repeatedly, they asked me to write a book that is comprehensive on the subject—"one we can read after Syd Field and before Robert McKee"—that explains and describes the elements of craft in models for the analytical mind, but offers a pathway into the layers of the process for writers of all levels. I was training them to do more than write a screenplay, I was opening their minds to *the mysteries of storytelling,* guiding them through the journey of *becoming a storyteller.* I was leading them through the critical and creative thinking tools that are required *to enter the process,* first and foremost, by establishing core human values, or moral values, inside the story. As most screenwriters know, the psychology of screenwriting involves problem-solving through diverse mental strategies, including vertical thinking, lateral thinking, creating character choices, making decisions, putting ideas on hold, assessing aesthetic nuances, organizing structure, creating flow charts and story boards, suggesting patterns and probabilities, and creating a *story spine* that explains those patterns. Then, there is that all-important human capacity we call empathy that allows us to identify with the inner story of the main character as we are writing it. However, what gives a story its universal appeal and emotional depth is the writer's ability to speak to the human heart *through the inner story* to convey *a larger idea that appeals to our humanity* as human beings.

A screenplay must be clear, complete, concise, correct, and consistent, but the process of *Screenwriting Is Storytelling* is filled with examples depicting the chaos of the human condition juxtaposed against our core human values. Creating this sophisticated dynamic requires developing tools for critical and creative thinking, and one of my personal objectives in writing this book is to share my discoveries by defining the creative avenues of the storytelling process and to offer easy access to these pathways for all writers.

Experienced screenwriters often ask me what I have learned by working with icons such as Tennessee Williams and Jason Miller, compared to working with beginners and preprofessionals. The truth is that experienced screenwriters make the same mistakes as beginners . . . they just hide them better!

BECOMING A STORYTELLER

Screenwriting Is Storytelling is meant to give you the foundation and tools necessary to develop your talent as a storyteller so you know how to get to the heart of the story intuitively and structurally as a screenwriter.

Storytellers know that screenwriting is a challenge. They know what their story is about before they begin, and as they work through plot and character-driven structure, they gradually discover the layers within their story. Storytellers long to be geniuses, but if they are really smart they remain storytellers *who are fascinated by human behavior* so they can characterize simple truths in stories.

....

Creating an A-List screenplay means telling a powerful story.
Powerful stories help us understand life.
The most talented actors are attracted to stories that speak
to all generations.

....

Part One: SCREENTHINKING: "What is my story about?" introduces the storyteller to the process of firsthand discovery, and the many aspects of critical and creative thinking behind this process. Storytellers begin by asking questions like "What is a story?" "Is there a formula?" "Is there a secret to the magic?" They also ask "Why do people go to movies?" "What do people want to see?" "What characters do people want to see?" "How can I create them?"

Part Two: SCREENPLANNING: "How does my story make the audience feel?" prepares you, as the storyteller, for planning your screenplay by defining "story" in behavioral terms based on *what it makes the audience feel*.

Part Three: SCREENWRITING: "This is what my story is about." Writing the all-important "one-page" summary of your story is the first step in defining what your story is about.

Part Four: REWRITING AND SCRIPTDOCTORING: "What is my story *really* **about?"** This stage is about refining the essence of your story, bringing it into focus, and defining its subconscious truth, so that you can create a movie that others will never forget. It involves rethinking and clarifying your story, again in behavioral terms.

Part Five: BREAKING IN AND STAYING THERE is an art form in and of itself. This section introduces you to www.breakingin.net, one of the most popular screenwriting websites on the Web that links screenplay competitions, scriptwriter networks, and other important websites such as The Writers Guild of America (www.wga.org) and Internet Movie Database (www.imdb.com) and introduces you to the business side of screenwriting.

Before we begin, let's establish one rule: When it comes to storytelling, *truth is everything.* Truth is simple. Absolute truth is simple, yet fully comprehensive. Getting to the absolute truth means we have much to learn from our own stories; to reach this level of poetic insight, we must let go of our own false notions and assume that audiences are smarter than we are. That's how we stretch our talent. That's how we find things people want to see. That's how we test our ideas and concepts to see if they work as films. That's how we approach story. That's how we create spine. That's how we understand inner story. That's how we experience spontaneous, meaningful insight. More importantly, that's how we enter the magnificent world of storytelling.

PART ONE

Screenthinking

"What is my story about?"

CHAPTER ONE

Screenwriting Is Storytelling

SCREENWRITING is storytelling. Storytellers are compelled to tell their stories—not necessarily for fame or fortune—but because their stories portray characters whose experiences help us understand our lives, define our core values, and reveal simple truths about life itself. Screenwriters are storytellers. Great screenwriters are great storytellers.

There is a constant demand for writers who can create good stories, especially for the big screen. However, there is an even a greater supply of stories and screenplays that don't work and will never make it to the screen. In fact, there are over one hundred thousand scripts written every year, and only a few hundred actually make it. Even then, most of these movies do not succeed. Usually the script is the culprit, and the most common script problem is lack of story.

Believe it or not, enormous attention is given to the process of developing good stories and screenplays for the big screen, but these statistics are startling proof of just how difficult it is to create a good story, let alone become a storyteller.

WHAT IS STORY?

Story creates the deeper understanding about human nature that we experience when we hear or see what has happened to another human being. Whether it's an incident in the life of someone we know, the true-life experience of someone in the news, the adventures of a fictional character, or the heroic life of a compelling historical figure, we are fascinated by the progression of events that a human being encounters, and this progression of events is called *plot*. However, what engages our imagination on a human level is how the main character reacts to this progression of events, and this cumulative insight is called *story*.

Story and plot are intricately woven inside story events, and while the audience cannot tell them apart, each is distinct: Plot is self-evident, and we experience it objectively, scene by scene. Story is the deeper meaning behind the plot, and we subjectively infer its moral truth—or absolute truth—sequentially, by identifying with the inner moral struggle of the main character.

Plot defines who, what, when, where, how, and why.
Story reveals the absolute truth.

What is a good story?

A good story features a main character, or protagonist, who confronts a strong moral choice. This is true in comedy as well as drama, and the main character is often referred to as a *classic hero*. The best stories feature a hero who struggles with his human flaws, and the story supports, negates, and challenges the hero's moral choice, or conflict, from the beginning, through the middle, until the very end.

The process of storytelling begins with a simple idea, a complex hero, and a compelling situation, giving all the elements of who, what, when, where, how, and why. The story progresses as the hero confronts opposing characters and faces a strong moral conflict, which must:

1) test his character, 2) reveal his flaws, 3) reflect universal values, and 4) become more difficult as the hero confronts the story complication.

The story complication is more than an obstacle or an idea; it is a major story event—a conceptual plot point that personifies the main character's internal struggle and challenges his or her conflict both internally and externally. The plot point is *conceptual* in that it opposes the compelling situation, and spins the story forward. Storytellers call this *the story twist.* When confronted with the story twist, the hero, despite all difficulties, reevaluates his moral choice, and takes the more difficult path into the *world where the story takes place.*

....

The story complication is a major story event
that opposes the compelling situation and challenges the
protagonist's moral struggle.

....

Storytellers are patient, and they know that developing the story twist is only the beginning of the storytelling process, because a good story is developed on several levels:

• The main character's outward goal, which sometimes is called the hero's mission

• The unconscious story that reflects the main character's internal conflict

• The onscreen relationship(s) that reveals the main character's emotional life

• The unity of emotional understanding, *or synthesis,* of the main character's internal transformation together with what the story is about.

STORYTELLERS VS. SCREENWRITERS

Outwardly, the storyteller holds the audience's interest by building toward the story's climax, with opposing characters, twists, turns, obstacles, surprises, victories, and defeats. Inwardly, however, the audience identifies with the hero's moral struggle, so the storyteller reveals the deeper meaning of the story through the hero's internal conflict.

At the moment when the hero's personal conflict merges with what the story is about—sometimes called the *synthesis of the story* or the *moment of realization*—the hero understands his own difficulties that he has overcome, and the audience—completely identifying with the hero's struggle—comes to a deeper understanding of the values and feelings surrounding the hero, how he has been morally tested, where he has succeeded, and how his journey reflects our own humanity.

At the story climax, the fully integrated classic hero overcomes all odds, externally defeats the opposing character(s), and resolves all story complications, giving the audience an emotionally satisfying experience.

Classic Screen Heroes

Classic screen heroes such as those played by John Wayne in *Rio Grande* (as Lt. Col. Kirby York) and *Stagecoach* (as The Ringo Kid), Gary Cooper in *High Noon* (as Marshal Will Kane) and *Mr. Deeds Goes to Town* (as Longfellow Deeds), Clark Gable in *It Happened One Night* (as Peter Warne) and *Mutiny on the Bounty* (as Lt. Fletcher Christian), and Harrison Ford in *The Fugitive* (as Dr. Richard Kimble) and *Air Force One* (as President James Marshall) convey powerful moral figures who overcome odds. Many of the most successful or compelling movies ever made feature a classic hero: *Titanic, Star Wars, To Kill a Mockingbird, Harry Potter and the Sorcerer's Stone, Spiderman, Independence Day, The Lion King, E.T.: The Extra Terrestrial, Forrest Gump, Return of the Jedi, Armageddon, Mission: Impossible,* and *The Empire Strikes Back.*

OTHER STORY FORMS

Classic screen heroes are not the only leading characters that can embody the story and create a powerful effect by featuring an intense character transformation. Other story forms speak to the audience through the main character's complex moral struggle.

Anti-Hero Story

The anti-hero adheres to his own personal code of honor, rather than society's. His moral code, however, remains steadfast, which is why audiences identify with his struggle. The word *moral* refers to natural law, as opposed to natural selection.

> Natural law is the code of behavior that arises in the absence of man's law.
> Natural selection is behavior that results from the survival of the fittest.
> Storytelling reflects the conflict between natural law and natural selection.

Moral code, therefore, is immutable, even as society's view of honor and ethics evolves from generation to generation. Americans, in particular, love individualism, which is why actors/characters who are known as antiheroes, Humphrey Bogart in *Casablanca* (as Rick Blaine) and *The Maltese Falcon* (as Sam Spade), Steve McQueen in *The Getaway* (as Carter "Doc" McCoy) and *The Thomas Crown Affair* (as Thomas Crown), Marlon Brando in *On the Waterfront* (as Terry Malloy), Gene Hackman in *The French Connection* (as Jimmy "Popeye" Doyle), and Clint Eastwood in *Unforgiven* (as William Munny), are immensely popular.

Faustian "Deal with the Devil" Story

The Faustian non-hero follows his base animal instincts, completely ignoring a code of honor or society's moral order. What makes this story form appealing is that the non-hero literally makes a deal with an evil force with a diabolical nature. However, we not only understand why the non-hero makes this choice, we actually identify with him as he overthrows the moral order. In fact, we enjoy watching him enter his world of emotional torture and personal turmoil, a world of his own making where he loses his job, his family, his status, his children, his soul, and all that is precious to him that could have been protected by following the moral order, or at the minimum, a code of honor and decency. Michael Douglas in *Fatal Attraction* (as Dan Gallagher) is the quintessential Faustian non-hero. Others include Robert DeNiro in *Raging Bull* (as Jake LaMotta), Richard Attenborough in *Jurassic Park* (as John Hammond), and Tom Cruise in *The Firm* (as Mitch McDeere). By the story's end, the Faustian characters recognize the error of their ways and return to their life renewed in spirit.

Redemption Story

The redemption story begins with a character who is deeply flawed and thrives on his ability to selfishly manipulate everyone around him. Then, something profound happens that changes his life forever, and he spends the rest of his life making every effort humanly possible to make up for his errant ways, to rectify a situation or right a moral wrong—in effect, to redeem his soul. Sometimes the redemption relates to a larger social issue such as civil rights or a compelling situation such as rescuing the world from destruction. *Schindler's List*, *Die Hard*, *The Shawshank Redemption*, *Amadeus*, *The Elephant Man*, and *The Quiet Man* are some of the most powerful redemption stories.

Buddy Story

The buddy story features two opposing characters who are forced to become friends, usually to work against a common enemy or to achieve an overreaching goal. Each is dependent on the other, and often there is a love-hate bond that is tested throughout the story. In the end, each goes his or her own way with triumphant feelings about their accomplishment, and mixed feelings about each other. Popular buddy stories include Paul Newman (as Butch Cassidy) and Robert Redford (as the Sundance Kid) in *Butch Cassidy and the Sundance Kid*, Mel Gibson (as Martin Riggs) and Danny Glover (as Roger Murtaugh) in *Lethal Weapon*, Bette Midler (as Sandy Brozinsky) and Shelley Long (as Lauren Ames) in *Outrageous Fortune*, John Travolta (as Vincent Vega) and Samuel L. Jackson (as Jules Winnfield) in *Pulp Fiction*, Peter Falk (as Vincent Ricardo) and Alan Arkin (as Sheldon Kornpett) in *The In-Laws*, and Chris Tucker (as Det. James Carter) and Jackie Chan (as Chief Inspector Lee) in *Rush Hour*.

Coming-of-Age Story

The story of a teenager(s) experiencing shades of adulthood for the first time and overcoming parental bonds is popular to all audiences, but especially to younger moviegoers. *American Graffiti*, *The Last Picture Show*, *Grease*, *Diner*, *Stand by Me*, and *The Breakfast Club* have captured the pulse of their respective generations. Although based on a vintage comic book, the immensely popular *Spiderman* speaks to a new generation about coming of age.

Female-Driven Story

The female-driven story can be difficult to sell to the worldwide market, which explains why the success of this type of movie can sometimes be more dependent on the status of the female movie star than on the quality of the story itself. In fact, those that endure usually include a strong romantic male lead that contrasts with the formidable female protagonist. Vivian Leigh (as Scarlett O'Hara) and Clark Gable (as Rhett Butler) in *Gone With the Wind,* Meryl Streep (as Karen Blixen) and Robert Redford (as Denys Hatton) in *Out of Africa,* Melanie Griffith (as Tess McGill) and Harrison Ford (as Jack Trainer) in *Working Girl,* Julia Roberts (as Vivian Ward) and Richard Gere (as Edward Lewis) in *Pretty Woman,* and Renee Zellweger (as Bridget Jones) and Colin Firth (as Mark Darcy) in *Bridget Jones's Diary* demonstrate the importance of on-screen romance with a handsome movie star. However, pure female-driven stories are moving upwards at the box office with successes such as *Erin Brockovich, Lara Croft: Tomb Raider, Charlie's Angels, Steel Magnolias, The Joy Luck Club, First Wives Club, Sophie's Choice, Norma Rae,* and *Alien.*

Love Story

Love stories appeal to old and young alike. A classic, epic love story requires a major conflict that keeps the lovers apart. What stands in their way often involves heroism, war, love of one's country, or the greater good of others, which are the only true reasons for lovers to give up their passion for one another. *Titanic, Casablanca, Gone With the Wind,* and *Dr. Zhivago* are classic epic love stories, as opposed to *It Happened One Night, An Affair to Remember, Love Story,* and *Ghost,* which are among the most popular romantic love stories wherein the lovers reunite at the end. Ironically, the greater the obstacles that keep the lovers apart, the more memorable the movie and the bigger the box office hit.

Ensemble Story

The ensemble story involves a hero and his entourage. It is theme-centered, as opposed to hero-centered. The ensemble is brought together in a mission or caper that requires the abilities of all participants, and consequently, tests the character traits of all participants. Examples include *The Dirty Dozen, The Big Chill, The Usual Suspects, L.A. Confidential, Ocean's Eleven,* and *The Lord of the Rings: Return of the King.*

WHAT STORYTELLERS KNOW ABOUT STORYTELLING

Storytellers know that a good movie is more than a good story with a good plot. A good movie takes us to an exciting new world—not just a visually interesting new world—a new world that is original, and that means, never been seen before.

Storytellers also know that there are no secret formulas to creating an original story, but it is essential to create a *dramatic situation* that reveals a compelling *moral dilemma,* and develop the moral choice with a *story complication* that renders the internal moral conflict even more difficult.

Discovery vs. Learning: Envy, Jealousy, and Greed

Although storytelling is about discovery, it begins with learning. All great stories feature at least one of three elements, especially in the relationship between the protagonist and the antagonist: *envy, jealousy, or greed.*

....

The character that opposes the protagonist is called the
antagonist.
If the protagonist is a classic hero, the antagonist is filled with
envy, jealousy, and greed.

....

Envy has nothing to do with love, and has everything to do with hate. If you have something I want, I will have to kill you to get it. Or, I'll take it away and spoil it so you won't have it. Also, it's not enough that I succeed; you must fail. Envy is a marvelous basis for the villain or antagonist who seeks to destroy the hero in order to prevail over a culture or civilization. In larger terms, the hero must defeat the envious villain, not only for his own survival, but most often in story terms, also for the greater good of mankind.

Jealousy is based on the notion of love, and a feeling of pain and hatred toward someone who takes away someone you love. We have a powerful identification with a hero who may be suffering feelings of jealousy due to loss of a loved one, and we can identify with the notion of defeating a rival, or antagonist, who must be rendered powerless so the hero can reclaim what is rightfully his.

Greed is the desire to have all the good stuff. It's a twisted form of ambition. The problem is that this emotion doesn't know when to stop and can destroy not only the ambitious and greedy, but those who are exploited by him. The greedy antagonist(s) must be stopped by a hero who is strong enough to defeat them and willing to risk his life to defend innocent people who cannot fend for themselves.

Originality

Storytellers know that all human beings use their unique talent to build creative ideas, and that all great artists unite their talents with originality. The important thing to keep in mind is that creativity comes from having a unique voice and acquiring the disciplines needed to express that creativity.

Creative genius is possible for all human beings.

In other words, originality of expression is innate to us as human beings, such that creative genius is possible for all human beings, especially those willing to master the analytical disciplines and creative avenues of storytelling.

CHAPTER TWO

Movies Are Entertainment

MOVIES are not literature. Movies are entertainment. The word *entertainment* comes from the Latin word *teneo,* which means *to hold,* as in *holding attention in the mind.* Entertainment must engage us, not merely as diversion or amusement, but by captivating our imagination and holding our interest on the fundamental human level. Before we consider what movies people want to see, let's ask:

WHY DO PEOPLE GO TO MOVIES?

1. *To escape their everyday lives.* People seek to experience adventure in an exciting world, a place where they have never been. By far, escapism is the most popular reason people go to movies. That's why popcorn, candy, and soda are big sellers at the concession stand: They comfort us in a childlike way so we can enjoy the escapism experience.

2. *To see a movie star.* People like to identify with movie stars. Seeing them light up the screen is the second most popular reason why people go to movies. In fact, some moviegoers actually believe that *movie stars are the larger-than-life characters* they see on screen.

3. *To experience the life of someone extraordinary.* People enjoy watching a sweeping biographical drama set in extraordinary times, featuring someone facing insurmountable obstacles, experiencing sorrows, losses, setbacks, sharing in their achievements, participating in their failures, and reconciling the lessons they learn about life, which they can apply to their own.

4. *To experience the internal struggle of someone ordinary.* Watching an ordinary person facing an extraordinary problem is a more subtle reason people go to movies, but a popular one, nonetheless.

5. *To reconcile our failings through catharsis.* People like to recognize human failures and foibles as internal conflicts in others, vicariously seeking reconciliation from personal and moral shortcomings in their own lives.

6. *To laugh at ourselves so we feel relieved of our personal struggles.* Movies are recession-proof. People go to movies in good times, and especially in bad times. During the Great Depression, Charlie Chaplin became a national hero. Steve Martin, Jim Carrey, Adam Sandler, and Will Ferrell haven't quite achieved icon status, but Billy Crystal, the perennial host of the Academy Awards, unites the globe with movie humor.

7. *To satisfy our human need for myths, stories, and legends.* Human beings have a deep spiritual need to connect with their poetic nature, and the storytelling process allows us to experience those feelings. In the past, ancient myths, Bible stories, folktales, and legends reassured mankind with stories wherein Good triumphs over Evil. Today, we look to movies to define our *universal values* that help us understand life.

WHAT MOVIES DO PEOPLE WANT TO SEE?

The industry standard for determining what movies people want to see is called the "box office." Box office gross receipts are reported in the millions of dollars. The top twenty all-time highest-grossing movies, including recent box office hits such as *The Passion of the Christ, Spider-Man 2,* and *Harry Potter and the Prizoner of Azkaban* reflect a long-term trend of hit movies that feature the triumph of good over evil. Another noteworthy trend is the appeal of movies that feature completely original visuals, stunts, and special effects, as the success of sequels (*The Lord of the Rings, Harry Potter, Shrek,* and *Spider-Man*) suggest.

THE TOP 20 MOVIES WORLDWIDE
STUDIO BOX OFFICE RECEIPTS
(Gross in $millions as of . . . 2004)

Titanic, 1997	$1,835.4
The Lord of the Rings: The Return of the King, 2003	1,069.6
Harry Potter and the Sorcerer's Stone, 2001	975.8
The Lord of the Rings: The Two Towers, 2002	926.1
Star Wars: The Phantom Menace, 1999	924.5
Jurassic Park, 1993	914.7
The Lord of the Rings: The Fellowship of the Ring, 2001	870.9
Harry Potter and the Chamber of Secrets, 2002	869.4
Finding Nemo, 2003	861.7
Spider-Man, 2002	821.6
Independence Day, 1996	817.0
E.T.: The Extra-Terrestrial, 1982	792.8
The Lion King, 1994	783.8
Star Wars, 1977	775.4
The Matrix Reloaded, 2003	783.6
Forrest Gump, 1994	679.7
The Sixth Sense, 1999	672.8
Pirates of the Caribbean, 2003	653.9

| *Star Wars: Attack of the Clones*, 2002 | 649.5 |
| *Lost World*, 1997 | 618.6 |

AMERICAN HEROES AND UNIVERSAL VALUES

Virtually all of these top twenty box office mega-hits are American-made movies; and although not all these films are set in America, they all portray classic heroes who *represent American ideals and universal values*, and their stories are presented in simple terms with epic proportions that take us to *exciting worlds we have never seen before.*

Titanic

A romantic epic about the power of love, this story features one man's choice to sacrifice his life for the sake of others, and let go of his true love who waits a lifetime to rejoin him for eternity. What makes *Titanic* the most popular movie of all time is the compelling journey Jack Dawson (Leonardo DiCaprio) takes into the world of the *Titanic* where the temporal nature of man—complete with dreams, desire, human sacrifice, false pride, and hubris—is played out in a time of life-threatening crisis. Before Jack even boards the ship, we know it is going to go down; nonetheless we go along for the journey because we want to enter this world and experience the dramatic feelings connected to eternal love, both romantic and selfless.

The Lord of the Rings: The Return of the King

The conclusion of *The Lord of the Rings* showcases the marathon battle for Middle Earth while Frodo (Elijah Wood) and Sam (Sean Astin) approach Mount Doom to finally rid their world of the One Ring. The record-breaking success of the first two films assured major box office, but what makes this film the most satisfying of the three installments—and Academy Award–winning Best Picture of the Year—were not just its outstanding special effects, but the timeless battle of good versus evil engaged in an epic war that echoes our own confounding times.

Harry Potter and the Sorcerer's Stone

This mega-family-appeal story about a boy named Harry (Daniel Radcliffe) who becomes a wizard, teaches us that success requires teamwork, talent, and virtue. What makes it an exciting movie that appeals to all ages are its bright, original characters and visual extravaganza of Harry's fanciful, imaginative, and powerful world of magic.

The Lord of the Rings: The Two Towers

Part two of *The Lord of the Rings* trilogy finds the fellowship broken, with Frodo and Sam journeying to Mordor to destroy the One Ring, while their former companions join forces with new partners to commence an attack on Isengard. What makes this a mega-hit among moviegoers is the inspired thematic adaptation by screenwriters who convey the unity of the forces of goodness toward a worthy purpose, pleasing loyal fans and attracting new admirers to the fold.

Star Wars: Episode I: The Phantom Menace

This is a story about discovering the truths about those we love. It also taps into moviegoers' desires to understand the origins of *Star Wars* characters, especially what drove Anakin Skywalker (Jake Lloyd), Luke's father, to the Dark Side of The Force to become Darth Vader. Like the original *Star Wars*, what makes it a great movie is the promise that good triumphs over evil amid the visual spectral of the intergalactic world.

Jurassic Park

This morality tale features a proud scientist (Sam Neill) who plays God as he pursues fame and fortune, and through tragedy, he is forced to accept his limitations and see his place in the balance between man and nature. What makes it a compelling movie is the unforgettable world of the spectacular park where dinosaurs rule.

The Lord of the Rings: The Fellowship of the Ring

This is a mythic story of how an unlikely hero named Frodo Baggins (Elijah Wood) sets out to defeat a dark power. If Frodo and his comrades practice fidelity, friendship, and honor, they can overcome the power that threatens to destroy their world. What makes it an extraordinary movie is the fantastic world of original characters and settings wherein the Fellowship risk their lives in a classic battle of good against evil.

Harry Potter and the Chamber of Secrets

Harry (Daniel Radcliffe) and his friends face new challenges in their second year at Hogwarts School of Witchcraft and Wizardry as they uncover a dark force that is terrorizing their school, involving petrified bodies. In addition to lavish sets and special effects, what makes it such a grand adventure story is Harry's loyalty to Hogwarts and his friendship with Ron (Rupert Grint) and Hermione (Emma Watson) as they uncover magical clues that restore safety and security to their beloved school.

Finding Nemo

This is the story of a free-spirited young fish named Nemo, who in an attempt at independence, separates from his fretful father fish Marlin, and is suddenly captured by a deep-sea fisherman and put in a fish tank at a dentist's office. Nemo and his father both embark on treacherous journeys in order to reunite. *Finding Nemo* is one of the most successful animated films of all time, not only due to the stunning visuals of the underwater world, but because of the touching portrayal of the universal experience of the pain and the glory of the parent-child relationship.

Spider-Man

A secret do-gooder (Tobey Maguire) uses his power with great responsibility, and ultimately gives up the affection of his ladylove for the greater good of mankind. What makes this film a box office delight is the visual presentation of becoming Spider-Man. By entering his virtual reality, we spring like Spider-Man, weaving webs throughout New York City, using extraordinary powers to defeat the evil ways of the Green Goblin (Willem Dafoe).

Independence Day

This futuristic tale features American heroes preserving American ideals, uniting the world, making it safe for democracy and overcoming the threats of the evil universe. What makes this a such a popular movie is the thrill of watching heroes fight valiantly for everything our country stands for, thereby giving audiences renewed appreciation for good over evil, and what it means to be American.

> Audiences are attracted to traditional themes and values that emphasize good, not evil.

E.T.:The Extra-Terrestrial

One of the most memorable films of all time, this heartwarming story is about finding home, learning to love, and connecting with family. What makes it a great movie is its simplicity, especially the magical creation of a boy's (Henry Thomas) enduring friendship with an extra-terrestrial—who literally takes him over the moon—and helps us to appreciate our own home and family.

The Lion King

An animated feature, this is the story of a lion cub who refuses to accept his father's legacy, but who ultimately rises to greatness through friendship, by taking responsibility for his people and leading them with courage, integrity, and affection. What makes it a satisfying movie is its visually appealing world of humanlike animals in the Lion King's jungle, where their survival depends on Simba taking on his role as leader of the tribe.

Star Wars

A young man, with the help of his friends, must trust in The Force, rescue Princess Leia (Carrie Fisher), and overcome Darth Vader in this now-classic morality tale of good versus evil. What makes it one of the most popular movies ever made is its one-of-a-kind visually stimulating intergalactic world of *Star Wars*.

The Matrix Reloaded

This science fiction piece is the story of a man named Neo—which means *the new man* in Greek—(Keanu Reeves) who must die to be resurrected by Trinity (Carrie-Anne Moss). Neo, however, has no idea who he is when the story begins, nor where he is, until Morpheus (Laurence Fishburne) extracts him from the Matrix to prepare him for his destiny. This is much more than a celebration of special-effects. This movie speaks to modern-day audiences as an allegory of the story of the Gospels.

Forrest Gump

An ordinary man (Tom Hanks) with frailties and disabilities experiences an epic journey through America's history. Because of his depth of compassion for others, he survives with dignity and hope, and provides a future for his child. What makes it one of the most beloved movies of all time is Forrest Gump's ability—against all odds, from generation to generation—to remain loyal and compassionate toward his mother (Sally Field), his childhood sweetheart (Robin Wright Penn), his child, and ultimately his beloved America, to become an epic hero for modern times.

The Sixth Sense

This touching story is about a boy (Haley Joel Osment) who is cursed with a gift to see the dead, and the child psychologist (Bruce Willis) who tries to help him. What makes it a fascinating movie is the startling experience of seeing the world through a different perspective, one that defies time and space and reminds us that life is precious and finite.

Pirates of the Caribbean: The Curse of the Black Pearl

Rogue pirate Jack Sparrow (Johnny Depp) teams with young Will Turner (Orlando Bloom) to regain control of his ship and to save a governor's daughter from the clutches of the evil Captain Barbossa (Geoffrey Rush). What makes this film a smash hit is the combination of a sweeping period romance with swashbuckling antics, breathtaking action sequences, and above all, the larger-than-life character of Jack Sparrow, whose original flair captivates our imagination.

Star Wars: Episode II: Attack of the Clones

Set ten years after the *Phantom Menace,* Jedi Knights Obi-Wan Kenobi (Ewan McGregor) and Anakin Skywalker (Hayden Christensen) discover there is more than meets the eye behind an assassination attempt on the life of Senator Padmé Amidala (Natalie Portman). At the crux of the story is a separatist movement led by a former Jedi (Christopher Lee) who incites a civil war in the Galactic Republic. This extravaganza of special effects, like the other Star Wars installments, portrays a story about good vs. evil—but this time from within the galaxy itself.

Lost World

This is the sequel to *Jurassic Park* in which the surviving dinosaurs are discovered to be more dangerous, fierce, and brutal than imagined. What makes it a megahit at the box office is the terrifying discovery that despite man's ingenuity and intellect, these dinosaurs have the ability to seek revenge and threaten man's existence.

OTHER "TOP MOVIES EVER WORLDWIDE"

Taking into account the rise in ticket prices over the last decade, there are other movies that deserve mention for their originality and appeal to mainstream audiences. Not only have they achieved major success at the box office, they remain among the all-time favorite movie rentals, loved by audiences throughout the world.

Men in Black

A stylish comedy about two secret agents (Will Smith and Tommy Lee Jones) assigned to keep tabs on earth-dwelling extra-terrestrials, the action comes to life when they must use their might and all their wits to save the world from destruction. What makes it a box office favorite is the contrasting world of the button-down, straight-laced Men in Black at odds with the hilarious, unpredictable world of the aliens.

Return of the Jedi

The conflict between good and evil plays out within Luke (Mark Hamill) as he resists the temptation of the Dark Side. He finally faces up to the truth about his father, Darth Vader, and with his father's help, destroys the Emperor. Ultimately, Luke is able to reconcile with his father, who is then released into Eternity to join The Force. What makes it a classic movie is that it exemplifies the triumph of good over evil, both in Luke and in the visually exciting intergalactic world of *Star Wars*.

Armageddon

Against an impossible eighteen-day time frame, a determined, heroic man (Bruce Willis) must drop a nuclear warhead inside a meteor before it destroys earth. What makes this film commercially appealing are its startling visual effects of the interplanetary world, where a meteor is about to destroy planet Earth, and the sheer determination of a man willing to risk his life for all mankind.

Mission: Impossible 2

An action-adventure secret agent hero (Tom Cruise) battles global criminals and terrorists with extraordinary valor, wit, and ingenuity. What makes this the ultimate "popcorn movie" is our immersion into the exciting world of visually original stunts where Tom Cruise outwits the bad guys and saves the day.

Home Alone

This family-appeal story features a boy (Macaulay Culkin) whose family leaves him behind for Christmas. He finds that his home, which represents his family, is worth fighting for, even if he has to do it alone. What makes this movie irresistible are the inventive antics of the boy who survives by his own wits and outlandish schemes that outsmart two goofy bad guys.

Ghost

This enduring love story is based on a powerful original concept about the enduring nature of romantic love. What makes it a mega-hit "date movie" is the inventive creation of the world of the occult and the promise of the afterlife as love's virtuous reward.

Terminator 2: Judgment Day

This is a story about human resistance against machines. The survivors of the nuclear fire called "Judgment Day" face an even greater nightmare, and the Terminator (Arnold Schwarzenegger), who keeps his promise ("I'll be back."), becomes a surrogate father to a young boy (Edward Furlong). What makes this one of the top science-fiction movies is the visually startling futuristic war against machines.

The Empire Strikes Back

This time Luke is called upon to save the galaxy, but realizes he needs the guidance of Yoda to become a Jedi Knight and defeat the Dark Side. What makes it a great movie, once again, is the visually exciting world of intergalactic wars where good triumphs over evil.

SPIRITUAL THEMES THAT BREAK THE BOX OFFICE

From time to time, studios undertake religious-based epics such as *The Ten Commandments, Gandhi,* and the animated feature *Prince of Egypt.* 2004 will be remembered as the year Mel Gibson risked it all to produce and direct *The Passion of the Christ,* starring Jim Caviezel as Jesus of Nazareth. The story focuses on the last twelve hours of Christ's life, opening in the Garden of Gethsemane where Christ resists temptation and is betrayed by Judas Iscariot (Luca Lionello). Arrested for blasphemy, he is condemned to death by crucifixion, and through his *passion,* we understand the *truth* of his life on earth . . . to love one another, especially our enemies, and to pray for those who persecute us. Although controversy surrounds this movie, its unexpected success at the box office speaks for itself. People need stories to understand life, especially stories that depict theologies and mythologies that offer a spiritual catharsis.

FALLEN HEROES AND DARK THEMES

Movies featuring fallen heroes and dark themes are not as successful at the box office. In fact, at the writing of this book only one made the list of "Top 100 Ever Worldwide": *American Beauty*, at number 100, with $336 million. *American Beauty* is a black comedy about a man whose family is falling apart as lust and ill fortunes take over his life. When he finally overcomes his personal peccadilloes, his life is cut short because of the conflicted lust of another man.

THE AMERICAN FILM INSTITUTE'S TOP AMERICAN FILMS OF THE 20TH CENTURY

The American Film Institute released its list of the Top American Films of the 20th Century in 2001; and although their choices do not necessarily represent the people's choice at the box office, these movies represent the film community's ongoing preference for complex heroes who face a strong moral choice in stories that reflect our core values and take us to exciting new worlds.

THE AMERICAN FILM INSTITUTE'S TOP AMERICAN FILMS OF THE 20TH CENTURY

Citizen Kane, 1941

Casablanca, 1942

The Godfather, 1972

Gone With the Wind, 1939

Lawrence of Arabia, 1962

The Wizard of Oz, 1939

The Graduate, 1967

On the Waterfront, 1954

Schindler's List, 1993

Singin' in the Rain, 1952

It's a Wonderful Life, 1946

Sunset Boulevard, 1950
The Bridge on the River Kwai, 1957
Some Like It Hot, 1959
Star Wars, 1977
All About Eve, 1950
The African Queen, 1951
Psycho, 1960
Chinatown, 1974
One Flew Over the Cuckoo's Nest, 1975

None of American Film Institute's Top Twenty American Films of the 20th Century explore themes relevant to the counterculture, but there are four of the top one hundred films that reflect it:

Bonnie and Clyde (1967), #27.

This glamorous movie portrays the true-life exploits of the notorious Depression-era bank robbers Bonnie Parker (Faye Dunaway) and Clyde Barrow (Warren Beatty), one a dreamer, the other a drifter. Together they celebrate their true love with crime, violence, and murder.

Midnight Cowboy (1969), #36.

The first X-rated film to win an Academy Award for Best Picture, this film tackles the corruption and cruelty of the New York City street scene through the unlikely friendship between a male prostitute (Jon Voight) who salvages his soul by restoring the humanity and dignity of a tubercular, homeless con artist (Dustin Hoffman).

Easy Rider (1969), #88.

This story features two motorcyclist misfits (Peter Fonda and Dennis Hopper) in search of real America, encountering the many faces of its big cities and small towns, a hippie commune, drugs, and sex in a New Orleans bawdy house. Although their lives are cut short, they make choices throughout the story that reveal their evolving humanity and capacity to honor their fellow man.

Pulp Fiction (1994), #95.

The story of a pair of low-rent hit men, one (John Travolta) who is assigned to entertain his boss's sexy wife, and the other (Samuel L. Jackson) his Bible-quoting partner. Together they find themselves on a wild ride of intrigue and corruption.

BIOGRAPHICAL EPIC

Biographical epics feature a true-life hero whose larger-than-life story is set against an historical event or era, which together reflect our shared history and core values.

THE TOP 10 BIOGRAPHICAL EPICS

Lawrence of Arabia, 1962
Schindler's List, 1993
Braveheart, 1995
Amadeus, 1984
Out of Africa, 1985
Gandhi, 1982
Reds, 1981
Patton, 1970
A Man for All Seasons, 1966
Ben-Hur, 1959

THE PULSE OF THEIR TIME

Storytellers pay attention to movies that capture the pulse of their time. Not only do these movies reflect the social mores of their time; these movies project social mores into future generations with memorable heroes and universal themes.

Movies That Captured the Pulse of Their Time

Chicago, 2003
Pretty Woman, 1990
When Harry Met Sally, 1989
Fatal Attraction, 1987
Top Gun, 1986
Tootsie, 1982
Saturday Night Fever, 1977
Annie Hall, 1977
Rocky, 1976
Jaws, 1975
The Sting, 1973
American Graffiti, 1973
Dr. Zhivago, 1965
The Sound of Music, 1965
The Searchers, 1956

FOREIGN FILMS

Storytellers appreciate films that originate outside America, especially those that reflect universal values through cultural differences and powerful characterizations:

Foreign Films That Spoke to the World

Lawrence of Arabia, 1962 (Britain, Columbia Pictures)
The Full Monty, 1997 (Britain, 20th Century Fox)
Four Weddings and a Funeral, 1994 (Britain, Gramercy Pictures)
Seven Samurai, 1954 (Japan, Criterion)
Chariots of Fire, 1981 (Britain, Columbia Pictures)

The Year of Living Dangerously, 1982 (Australia, Warner Bros.)
Crouching Tiger, Hidden Dragon, 2001 (Taiwan, Columbia Tristar)
Mad Max, 1981 (Australia, 20th Century Fox)
Life Is Beautiful, 1999 (Italy, Miramax)
Cinema Paradiso, 1990 (Italy, Miramax)
The 400 Blows, 1959 (France, Zenith International)

ACTION HEROES

The success of action heroes reflects the popularity of American heroes in the worldwide marketplace, and speaks for itself:

ACTION HEROES PROMISE ADVENTURE

True Grit, 1969 (John Wayne)
Casablanca, 1942 (Humphrey Bogart)
The Thomas Crown Affair, 1968 (Steve McQueen)
Dirty Harry, 1971 (Clint Eastwood)
James Bond Classics (Sean Connery, Roger Moore, Pierce Brosnan)
Rambo, 1987 (Sylvester Stallone)
Die Hard, 1988 (Bruce Willis)
Lethal Weapon, 1987 (Mel Gibson and Danny Glover)
Raiders of the Lost Ark, 1981 (Harrison Ford)
The Terminator, 1984 (Arnold Schwarzenegger)
Batman, 1989 (Michael Keaton)
Beverly Hills Cop, 1984 (Eddie Murphy)
Mission: Impossible, 1996 (Tom Cruise)

MOVIES WITH A "VOICE"

If the big box office ("boffo") movies mentioned above are not appealing to you, perhaps you belong to the rare breed of screenwriters and filmmakers who are more interested in creating *movies with a voice.* By voice, I mean that the tone and style of your work is unique to your own perspective and irresistible to a particular niche or following. This means that what you say *and how you say it* appeals to its own particular audience for its originality, but not necessarily the mainstream marketplace. This is a great gift, which can also be a curse. It may mean that you have to finance your movies through the independent market. The reward, of course, is when they succeed, you can continue making niche movies from independent sources:

WRITERS AND FILMMAKERS WITH A VOICE

Charlie Kaufman, *Being John Malkovich,* 1999

Nia Vardalos, *My Big Fat Greek Wedding,* 2002

Steve Martin, *Bowfinger,* 1999

Quentin Tarantino and Roger Avary, *Pulp Fiction,* 1994

Callie Khouri, *Thelma & Louise,* 1991

Colin Higgins, *Harold and Maude,* 1971

John Sayles, *Lone Star,* 1996

The Coen Brothers, *Fargo,* 1996

Spike Lee, *Do the Right Thing,* 1989

Woody Allen, *Annie Hall,* 1977

David Lynch, *Mulholland Drive,* 2001

WHAT ARE OUR CORE VALUES?

Filmmakers are always attracted to original ideas and stories, but storytellers struggle to portray the humanity inside the core values of our culture that, through profound characterizations, can also translate to the worldwide market:

• Sacrificing one's life for the greater good of mankind is the supreme heroic act.

• Sacrificing one's life to liberate innocent people from the tyranny of evil is a close second.

• Sacrificing one's life for love or to protect one's family is one of the strongest on-screen motivations.

• Letting go of your own romantic desire in favor of the greater good is another strong on-screen motivation.

• Loyalty to God and country, and family are the hallmarks of heroism.

• Home is love of family, one of our highest ideals.

• Romantic love endures forever, especially when lovers let it go.

• Pride is tragic, envy is deadly, but vengeance leads to eternal damnation.

• Heroes make difficult choices: courage over cowardice, fidelity over betrayal, humility over pride, forgiveness over vengeance.

• Shadow heroes escape the sunlight. Their heroic deeds are known only to themselves, which is why they become our most beloved heroes.

WHAT VALUES AM I ATTRACTED TO?

Freedom. Sacrifice. Liberty. Justice. Loyalty. Tyranny. Greed. Envy. Jealousy. Betrayal. Choose wisely. Exploring values is the essence of storytelling.

People need stories to understand life.

CHAPTER THREE

The Big Idea

CREATING a big idea for a movie is like falling in love. You know it when you feel it. You know it when you hear it. You know it when you see it. You know it because you'd be willing to stake your career on it.

IS IT ORIGINAL?

One of the most difficult things to communicate to screenwriters is the value of patience when it comes to creating an idea big enough for a movie. In the interests of moving ahead quickly, they settle on a pretty good idea and end up imitating other movies instead of taking the time to develop a big idea that is 100 percent original. It's true that we all like to "feel familiar" with the genre or underlying theme of a story, but if the big idea is not original or fascinating enough for a movie, then the story never takes off.

In the same vein, one of the most exciting aspects of screenwriting is the challenge of coming up with a handful of big ideas and taking the time to choose which idea lends itself not only to a story concept, but a movie for the big screen.

As a general rule, you might begin with a dozen ideas, eliminate the weak ones, and narrow your list down to three or four big ideas. You will find there is usually one that stays with you, but even with seeming certainty, don't jump yet. It is important to recognize that there are an infinite number of good ideas and a finite amount of time—so it's your job to come up with one or two big ideas and spend your time wisely! When you find yourself suffering from "story-block" the following are a few avenues that are fertile ground for getting you started.

The Interesting World

Movies take us where we have never been before, so the world where the movie takes place is crucial to creating a big idea that is 100 percent original. If you have the imagination to create an original, interesting world, this is your opportunity to shine. Or if you have a particular expertise or life experience in a unique profession, you may want to explore what you already know in the context of a story. In any case, take us into that special world where only you hold the key!

If you have a particular expertise, explore what you already know.

Fascinating Character

Movie stars like to play complex, fascinating characters with interesting moral dilemmas. It doesn't matter whether you create a completely original character, negotiate the life story rights of a living character based on a true story, or portray a larger-than-life historical figure: Make your character big, complex, and fascinating!

True Stories

Having developed many television projects based on true stories and several feature films as biographical epics, I always recommend working through proper channels (lawyers and estates) to acquire the releases pertaining to life story rights and/or rights to previously published material *before you begin*. No exceptions. In fact, entertainment law is a specialized practice of the law; and proper legal advice will help you define the "underlying rights" of the story, so you can address potential legal problems that may prevent you from getting an *Errors and Omissions* insurance policy, which investors require before production begins.

Studios and investors require insurance policies to protect their investment from mistakes that may have occurred in the area of rights and permissions.

This is known as an Errors and Omissions Policy.

Common mistakes in the area of rights and permissions include 1) underlying story rights, such as a short story, stage play, or book which is the basis of the screenplay, 2) life rights of a living person who is represented in the screenplay, or 3) authorship rights of another writer who of the script who has not been compensated. If any of these issues are not properly resolved, they constitute a "cloud" on the "chain of title" of the script, which prevents the movie from going forward to production.

If underlying story rights, life rights, or authorship rights cloud the "chain of title" of the script, insurance carriers will not issue an Errors and Omissions Policy.

True stories remain one of the best sources for movies and the list of "must read" newspapers and periodicals include *The New York Times, People Magazine, The Los Angeles Times, The Wall Street Journal,* and other major publications such as *Newsweek, Time,* or *Psychology Today.*

Public Domain

There are many stories, books, and historical events that are in the public domain, which means anyone can write a movie based on that subject matter without acquiring rights. If in doubt, always check with an attorney, film agent, or experienced producer who can guide you through the fundamentals of this specialized area of law. The last thing you want to do is to presume the story you have written is in the public domain, and after the script is written, discover that you do not own your script or that the underlying rights to your script are not available.

Incidents in the News Media

Sometimes there is an interesting true-life incident that isn't a movie, but contains a kernel of an idea that can be developed into a movie. There is a fine line here between a true story and an incident that inspires a fictional story, so if you plan to base a movie on a true-life incident you have read or seen in the media, it is a good idea to check with an entertainment lawyer or experienced literary agent before you begin. Also, remember that comedy often originates with incidents that capture our sense of the ludicrous. Spinning comedy out of current events is what makes *Saturday Night Live* so successful, so don't hesitate to look to the headlines for comedic material.

Medical Journals

Great stories can be created from interesting medical incidents and research, particularly for developing a medical techno-thriller. Psychiatric journals are also of interest because they recount the background of interesting cases, detailing human behavior that is unique and original.

True-Life Characters

Everybody has a favorite aunt, uncle, cousin, teacher, priest, rabbi, or next-door neighbor who is larger-than-life. Without featuring their actual life story or representing them personally as a true-life character, you can draw on them to create irresistible and remarkable character traits and behaviors that lend themselves to storytelling.

Interesting Legal Cases

Again, truth is stranger than fiction, and there may be a true story or kernel of an idea from an incident recounted in a lawsuit, with or without a complete story. You must consider whether the idea is big enough for a movie. Remember, wherever there is one lawsuit, there will be a minimum of two lawyers, or sets of lawyers, so you must consider that the lawyers represent the interests of their clients, whose life rights or release you may need to tell the story as a true story.

Scientific Journals

Anything that opens the human mind to the scope of the scientific world offers a major arena for a big idea. Journals such as *Scientific American* and *Nature* can inspire your imagination toward many intriguing possibilities, especially for science fiction. This is one of my favorite sources.

Forensic Cases

Everybody is fascinated by murder cases, especially when there is no body and no definitive cause of death. Agatha Christie created a world and a story around each and every case, and elevated this genre to an art form. Stay tuned to all the latest murder cases in the media and on Court TV. Somebody somewhere will always come up with one more ingenious way to commit the perfect murder and do away with the corpse, seemingly without any evidence.

IS IT A MOVIE POSTER?

Although this may seem like a dangerous shortcut as you are starting out, one of the strongest criteria for choosing a big idea to develop into a movie is to practice imagining the movie poster before you even decide to write the screenplay. Some posters feature only the title, as *For-*

rest Gump successfully demonstrated in its early marketing campaign. Others, such as *Mission: Impossible* involve a visual concept, the title, and the lead actor's name, especially if the star is someone of international stature like Tom Cruise. Most movie posters, such as *The Lord of the Rings: The Return of the King* feature the title and a visual concept. The best way to acquaint yourself with how to visualize your story into a single image is to study full-page newspaper ads. Marketing, advertising, and publicity departments expertly convey the fundamentals of storytelling in concise, visual terms. If you are able to conceptualize your idea into one powerful image that sparks the imagination, then you undoubtedly have a big idea for the big screen.

Once you have a few big ideas, you might try writing a one-page summary for each idea to see how it plays out in story form. This is where having a mentor or script coach is valuable, but it is wise to seek the judgment of someone reputable. Check out *www.breakingin.net,* a website that features interviews with established script coaches who are well known to the film community. If you cannot afford a script coach, try forming a writers' group where you can get feedback. Somewhere in this mix, there will be a consensus of opinion that will move you into the direction of committing to the *most original* big idea.

If you are the kind of person who prefers the development and execution of the story, as opposed to discovering or creating the big idea, then be patient. There are some individuals who are constantly filled with original ideas, but have trouble committing to developing or writing their ideas into stories. In such cases, there is no harm in partnering with another writer and creating something truly original together, based on your execution skills. My only caution is that eventually in a writing partnership, both writers have to contribute to the written page, so it's important to know that your writing partner has a surplus of original ideas as well as the drive to master the elements of story and the fundamentals of screenwriting.

People often ask me what makes a great writing partnership. In simple terms, do not choose your equal; choose someone whom you admire. That feeling must be mutual. When you work in the trenches together, you do not want to argue and defend your turfs, you want to complement each other and challenge each other to achieve higher levels of creativity. With mutual respect for each other's ability and talents, you will be able to create something extraordinary.

THE DRAMATIC SITUATION: IS IT COMPELLING?

Making your big idea work is like marriage. It begins with romance, but once you're committed, it requires hard work. This is where you have to set objective standards. Your big idea is going nowhere if you don't have a main character with a moral dilemma. Believe it or not, the most compelling element—testing the moral strength of the main character—sustains us throughout the entire story. Unless it is presented clearly in the first fifteen pages, you have no story potential for your big idea.

Creating a story complication is the next important phase, and usually this is where problems arise. Many screenplays have a big idea, strong dramatic situation, and the makings of a moral dilemma, but not enough complication from the antagonist and opposing forces to create a story concept that keeps us at the edge of our seats for the next one hundred pages.

TESTING YOUR STORY CONCEPT: IS IT A MOVIE?

Testing your story concept and spine are essential during the screen-thinking phase. If you think through the many possibilities before you begin, you will have the opportunity to rule out those story choices that may set you off in the wrong direction. Keep in mind the wrong direction in storytelling terms means settling for something derivative, predictable, and imitative—as opposed to creating something original, vibrant, and never seen before. Here is a quick checklist that I have developed with fellow writers to keep us from falling into those traps:

✓ What makes my story original *as a movie?*

✓ Is your story similar to another movie you have seen?

✓ Is there an original approach that makes the story irresistible?

✓ Compare your concept with movies that have failed.

✓ Compare your concept with movies that have succeeded.

✓ Compare your concept with the current marketplace.

✓ Know your story: Define what kind of story you want to tell.

✓ Give the lead character the most conflict.

✓ Give the lead character a compelling moral decision or dilemma.

✓ Play devil's advocate regarding your story and your movie.

✓ Define reasons *why not* to make your movie.

✓ Commit to a genre: Is the story best told as a sub-genre?

✓ On a daily basis ask yourself, "What is my story about?"

By applying these criteria as you work with your big idea, you will find that developing a story for a movie can be a fascinating endeavor. While it begins with a burst of enthusiasm, the next step is to open up the many possibilities within the idea by addressing the challenge of creating the story.

CHAPTER FOUR

The Four "Story" Questions

CREATING layers in storytelling often occurs unconsciously. The more levels there are to the characterizations, the more compelling the story. Although some levels are created intuitively in abstract terms, there are four concrete story questions you can—*and must*—ask yourself as you prepare to develop your story into a screenplay:

- What is the story?

- Whose story is it?

- What is the "key" to the story?

- From whose point of view is the story told?

WHAT IS THE STORY?

"What Is the Story?" is a loaded question. The person who asks it really means: "Tell me what happens in the story in such a way that I understand the meaning behind the events of the story." The listener wants a *short version of the events of the story* including some twists and turns, not a scene-by-scene breakdown. The listener also expects to hear which genre you will employ to tell this story.

In a classroom setting, the first assignment is to ask screenwriters to convey their stories on paper in a few hundred words. This exercise encourages them to become comfortable with telling their stories in as few words as possible. More importantly, it introduces them to storytelling— as problem-solving—so they can approach the creative process by asking questions.

WHOSE STORY IS IT?

In the world of movies, this question is usually asked in a different form: "Who can star in your movie?" The listener wants to know if you are writing a classic hero for someone like Harrison Ford, Ben Affleck, George Clooney, or Brad Pitt; whether you are writing an anti-hero for someone like Robert DeNiro, Michael Douglas, Sean Penn, or Kevin Spacey; or whether you are writing a character-leading man for someone like Jack Nicholson, Tommy Lee Jones, or Edward Norton. This question also probes the meaning of the story:

- In *Titanic,* it's Jack's story, as Rose's hero.

- In *The Fugitive,* it's the dual story of Dr. Richard Kimble and Officer Gerard.

- In *Tootsie,* it's Michael's story, even when he's dressed as Dorothy.

If you're writing a female-driven story, this question is paramount. Although it is best to create a story without regard to gender, the fact that there are fewer female stars who can carry a picture at the box office raises the "Whose story is it?" question in casting terms. Actors unconsciously represent specific character traits and arch-types, but when there are fewer to choose from in casting terms, as in a female-driven story, it benefits the project to address this issue early on. For example, is your leading lady complex and mysterious like Nicole Kidman, Charlize Theron, or Kate Winslet? Is she light and adorable like Julia Roberts, Kate Hudson, or Renee Zellweger? Or is she bold and comedic, in which case Catherine Zeta-Jones, Uma Thurman, or Cameron Diaz may be better choices.

WHAT IS THE "KEY" TO THE STORY?

Sometimes determining the "key" to the story can be very difficult. The "key" is usually found within the opposing forces of the story or in the antagonist who challenges the main character. In conceptual terms, the "key" also opens the story thematically. The central conflict that emerges within this question usually takes some time to discover, but once the excavation begins, the story opens up on numerous levels. It is helpful to think of this process as looking for a "key" that opens up the treasure chest of the ideas behind the story, which reveals multiple layers underneath.

• The "key" to *Titanic* is Rose's heart-shaped blue sapphire, which represents her love for Jack and her wish to be reunited with him through eternity.

• The "key" to *The Fugitive* is Officer Gerard's obligation to bring Dr. Kimble to justice, despite the consistently exculpatory evidence Gerard uncovers while doggedly pursuing Kimble.

• The "key" to *Tootsie* is Michael's romantic interest for Julie, which inspires him to become a better man, and Dorothy's character (Michael's alter ego), who emerges with goodness and generosity and attracts the affection of Julie's father, Les.

FROM WHOSE POINT OF VIEW IS THE STORY TOLD?

The point-of-view character fascinates screenwriters almost as much as spine. In literature, the point-of view character *tells the story*, and literally becomes the narrator. In film, the point-of-view character is the on-screen character that *reveals the story*. The point-of-view character leads the audience through the emotional story, and by interacting with the main character, enables the audience to follow the transformation of the main character. Paradoxically, the audience identifies with the main character's struggle; but in fact, the audience actually follows the struggle through another character within the story—the character with whom you, as the writer, are identified. Through external conflict, this dynamic character reveals the nuances and inner conflicts of the main character for the audience in such a way that the audience always understands what is going on inside the mind-set of the main character.

In film, the point-of-view character interacts
with the main character.

• In *Titanic,* it's Rose, with her wish to let go of all social and cultural obstacles that stand between her and Jack.

• In *The Fugitive,* it's cleverly split between Gerard and his investigative team who pursue Dr. Kimble. They function as a Shakespearean chorus, supporting and opposing Gerard's transformation that evolves as he uncovers contradictory and exculpatory evidence, which eventually exonerates Dr. Kimble.

• In *Tootsie,* it's the lovely Julie, a single mother, who thinks she understands Dorothy, but desperately needs to find a man she can love who can help raise her beautiful daughter with the same emotional security and refinement that her father, Les, has given her. When she realizes Dorothy is a man named Michael who has deceived her, she retreats from the friendship until Michael's transformation is complete.

Answering the four questions pertaining to story is essential to getting off to a good start. It is a terribly exciting way to begin because it opens up the story to a world of infinite possibilities. Don't shortchange yourself. Take your time with this process.

CHAPTER FIVE

Form: 3-Act Paradigms

WRITING a screenplay is a combination of form and process. Both can be learned, but one without the other is incomplete. Most screenwriters approach screenwriting as a craft, hoping to succeed by watching movies and relying only on formulas—that is, stories we have seen before that can be reduced to predictable formats, story points, and obligatory scenes. By focusing heavily on format, structure, and plot, screenwriters often underestimate the importance of discovering what the story is about, and shortchange their personal development as storytellers. Screenwriting form is meant to steer you in the right direction; however, the "right direction" really means expressing your personal voice and developing originality as a storyteller. Achieving this is a lifetime journey that begins with personal authenticity, and the ability to integrate creativity, both in form and process. Let's begin by reviewing the form of the Basic 3-Act Paradigm for a major motion picture screenplay, which was originally defined by Syd Field, Hollywood's most sought-after screenwriting teacher, in his landmark book, *Screenplay: The Foundations of Screenwriting*, which I recommend as required reading. Not only will it ground you in the discipline of what is required to write a motion picture screenplay for major studios, it will introduce you to the basics you need to begin preparing for the difficult journey of becoming a storyteller.

FORM: THE BASIC 3-ACT PARADIGM

A screenplay can be 120 pages, but today it is usually less than 110. It is a story that is told in a 3-Act Dramatic Structure, with a beginning, middle, and end. The key to dramatic structure is that there is one main character, called the protagonist, and that the protagonist's story builds as a "character-driven" story toward a climax.

The Set-Up

The first fifteen pages of the screenplay, which Syd Field defines as the set-up, introduce and establish everything that follows, and therefore, must include:

- ✓ Main character: also called the lead character or protagonist

- ✓ State of mind: the internal conflict of the protagonist

- ✓ The main character's ordinary world: the setting where the story begins

- ✓ Dramatic premise: also called the inciting incident, by page 3

- ✓ The world where the story takes place: where the story goes in Act II

- ✓ Dramatic situation: the basic idea of the story, usually by page 15

The Act I Plot Point

Between pages 25 and 35, the protagonist confronts the antagonist who opposes the protagonist and attempts to thwart the protagonist's goal or mission. This confrontation, which Field calls the *Act I plot point,* leads the protagonist to doubt his or her mission, but ultimately moves the protagonist forward into a world where the story takes place.

The Mid-Point Plot Point

Between pages 55 and 65, the protagonist is forced into the antagonist's world, thereby redefining the premise and situation, this time by the antagonist. Field calls this the *mid-point plot point.*

The Act II Plot Point

Between pages 72 and 85, the protagonist is defeated by the antagonist. Field calls this the *Act II plot point,* and this corresponds with the story point wherein the protagonist is nearly defeated and willing to abandon his mission.

The Ending

The last ten pages of the screenplay leads to the climax of the story when the protagonist comes to a deeper understanding of his experiences and defeats the antagonist. The resolution follows, wherein the protagonist quickly ties up all the loose ends of the story, and now that his character and values have been tested, he returns to his old world with a deeper understanding about life, changed forever.

SYD FIELD'S SCREENPLAY FORM				
The Set-Up	Act I Plot Point	Mid-Point	Act II Plot Point	The Ending
pages 1–15	pages 25–35	pages 55–65	pages 72–85	last 10 pages

STORY PROGRESSION

Although the story takes shape into a form that we may refer to as a "3-Act Structure," this paradigm is only the invisible form that that offers guidelines for story development—it is not story development. Storytellers think in terms of *story progression,* developing the main character's story against the forces of antagonism that drive the story. This is called *character-driven story structure.*

Storytelling requires surrendering to the exploration of the human condition. This means that you must be willing to let go of your own personal biases and limitations, and open up your mind to the possibilities of your story. It requires staying "on story"—focused on the main character as the driving force of the story—but experimenting with character behavior, supporting characters, and ideas that reveal your story with a unique, original voice.

> Storytellers explore the human condition through a unique,
> original voice.

Screenwriters often make the mistake of creating a plot, in lieu of developing their own personal voice as storyteller. They move along with exciting gimmicks, gizmos, and conceits, plotting them together logically, filling in the blanks, writing obligatory scenes, imitating genres, and ending up with a story that has no emotional center or a story that goes nowhere because it's not original.

THE ADVANCED 3-ACT PARADIGM

Storytellers internalize the guidelines of the 3-act structure, recognizing that creating the inner workings of the story, conflict, and characters is the task at hand. Creating story progression through character-driven structure can be so overwhelming that, over the years, I developed a more advanced 3-Act Paradigm that has been very successful with students and clients. It originates from working in the editing room as a producer, watching editors put movies together that were lacking story sequences, and in some cases, major story points. Not only does this paradigm feature the "12-Sequence-Story" that most screenwriters develop in a major motion picture screenplay, it features the twelve sequences in a 3-6-3 structure, with three sequences in the first act, six sequences in the second act, and three sequences in the third act. This paradigm also draws on elements of traditional storytelling as defined by Joseph Campbell and developed by Christopher Vogler; but more importantly, it includes secrets from extraordinarily gifted writers and film directors who have taught me how to develop characters that represent *emotional ideas* within the story that support the essence of the story, or what we, the audience, experience as the inner story.

Beware of taking this advanced paradigm, or any paradigm, as gospel! It is meant to be a framework to help you stay on track as you create a screenplay, as opposed to a recipe "how-to" imitate great screenplays. However, before you study this presentation, it is necessary to understand a few more basics about storytelling for film:

- A movie is a *series of shots* that are edited together to create *scenes,* which are edited together to create *sequences,* which are edited together to create the movie.

- A story in a screenplay is told in sequences, not scenes. A *sequence is a series of scenes,* with a beginning, middle, and end. Each sequence has its own major story point and climax; and each scene has its own separate climax that builds on the next scene climax toward the major story point and sequence climax. There are twelve sequences in a major motion picture screenplay, structured in a 3-6-3 3-act breakdown, all of which build toward the story climax. The number of scenes within each sequence varies from three to seven, but each sequence is roughly seven to fifteen pages. Each scene is about two pages long and is *series of shots, with a beginning, middle, and end.*

• From a basic story perspective, all story points are based on conflict, both internal and external, and each of the twelve sequences
has its own dramatic story point that builds sequence upon sequence. This sum total—called story progression—reveals character
through behavior, advances the story through conflict, explores the
theme through ideas, and creates an image through visuals as the
story as it moves to its climactic conclusion.

• From an advanced story perspective, each of the twelve sequences
explores a different aspect of what the story is about, and *through
human behavior, internal conflict,* and *external conflict,* reveals the
transformation of the protagonist into a fully integrated character,
or mature persona, which reflects a deeper meaning behind the story.

CREATING 12 SEQUENCES WITHIN 3-ACT STRUCTURE

Act I

Sequence 1 The set-up begins with introducing the protagonist, his
state of mind, and ordinary world, by establishing what storytellers call
the premise, or what Aristotle called the inciting incident, that triggers
the plot and the story. This event happens in the first few pages of the
screenplay, and takes place in the protagonist's ordinary world. Working with three contemporary films as examples, let's break down the
structure of their stories by sequence:

TITANIC
(1997, 20th Century Fox, Paramount Pictures, Lightstorm Entertainment)
Written by James Cameron
Producers: James Cameron, Pamela Easley Harris, Al Giddings, Grant Hill, Jon
    Landau, Sharon Mann, Rae Sanchini
Directed by James Cameron
The present day exploratory mission to recover the R.M.S. *Titanic,* the "unsink-
able" ship that sank to the bottom of the ocean on April 15, 1912, discovers an
erotic portrait of a young woman. A 101-year-old woman (Gloria Stewart)

identifies herself as Rose Dawson (Kate Winslet), the woman in the portrait, and steps forward to tell the story.

TOOTSIE
(1982, Columbia Pictures Corporation, Delphi, Mirage, Punch Productions, Inc.)
Story by Larry Gelbart and Don McGuire
Screenplay by Larry Gelbart and Murray Shisgal
Producer: Sydney Pollack, Dick Richards, Charles Evans
Directed by Sydney Pollack
Michael Dorsey (Dustin Hoffman), an out of work actor whose last job was playing a tomato, is a self-centered womanizer who barely appreciates the birthday surprise party that his girlfriend Sandy (Teri Garr) throws for him.

THE FUGITIVE
(1993, Warner Bros.)
Based on Characters by Roy Huggins
Story by David Twohy
Screenplay by Jeb Stuart and David Twohy
Producers: Arnold Kopelson, Keith Barish, Stephen Brown, Nana Greenwald,
    Peter MacGregor-Scott
Directed by Andrew Davis
Dr. Richard Kimble's wife (Sela Ward) is brutally murdered, and Dr. Kimble (Harrison Ford) is arrested as the prime suspect.

Within the next few pages, the storyteller establishes motivation for the main character, foreshadows the world where the story takes place, and reveals the dramatic situation of the story. Sophisticated writers also establish a point-of-view character—that is, a character within the story who represents the writer's own point-of-view throughout the story and offers an understanding of what the story is about. The point-of-view character is crucial to the movie-making process because in order to understand the story as a movie on-screen, the audience must understand the transformation of the main character. If there is no point-of-view character who helps the audience define this transformation, the audience does not have a dramatic anchor for the story on-screen, and consequently, does not know how to follow the inner emotional story. The other fundamental to keep in mind is that the *premise*, which triggers the story, occurs in the first few pages. This is the basis of the story concept, and through character conflict, the story builds on this premise, *revealing the dramatic situation*, which develops throughout the story toward the climax to the resolution:

TITANIC   Young Rose DeWitt Bukater (Kate Winslet) and her mother (Frances Fisher) board the "unsinkable" R.M.S. *Titanic* on April 14, 1912. Rose, who is smothered by her mother's ambition to marry her off into high society, is also oppressed by her wealthy, but controlling fiancé, Cal Hockley (Billy Zane). Meanwhile, Jack Dawson (Leonardo DiCaprio) is an adventurous American from Wisconsin who wins two tickets back to America on the *Titanic* in a poker game. He boards the ship along with over two thousand others, including an American named Molly Brown (Kathy Bates) and the shipbuilder, Mr. Andrews (Victor Garber), who receives a hearty welcome from Captain Smith (Bernard Hill). Jack lays eyes upon Rose for the first time as she gazes out into the sea. Her fiancé, Cal, interrupts her reverie, and Jack savors the view of the ocean from the bow of the magnificent ship, proclaiming, "I'm King of the World!"

TOOTSIE   Michael Dorsey preps his girlfriend, Sandy, to audition for the acting role of hospital administrator Emily Kimberly on a soap opera, *Southwest General,* which she loses because she's not tough enough. Michael, whose agent George tells him nobody will hire him, puts on a wig and a dress and auditions for the role as Dorothy Michaels.

THE FUGITIVE   Dr. Richard Kimble is arrested and interrogated by detectives who believe he murdered his wife for the proceeds of her life insurance policy. He is indicted and convicted of first-degree murder, and the presiding judge sentences him to death by lethal injection, with the admonition, "May God have mercy on your soul."

Sequence 2 The task here is to introduce the antagonist who opposes the protagonist, while revisiting the protagonist's motivation. Also, this is a great opportunity to reveal elements of the back-story that reflect the main character's state of mind and character flaw. Moreover, this is a chance to develop the antagonist as the point-of-view character, offering the audience an immediate window into the story.

TITANIC Rose, who has had enough of her socially ambitious mother and condescending fiancé, escapes from a formal dinner, and attempts to throw herself over the railings of the ship into the ocean. Jack, willing to risk his own life by jumping over to save her, offers her his hand. She slips and nearly falls, but he rescues her, only to be mistaken for a scoundrel who is molesting her. Rose, unwilling to admit the truth, offers enough of a tall tale so that Jack is judged to be a hero by Cal, who invites Jack to join them for dinner.

TOOTSIE Michael, as Dorothy, wins the audition for the irrepressible hospital administrator Emily Kimberly, and during his first day as a woman, loses a taxicab to a man who pushes her out of the way. Using a typically masculine solution, Michael, as Dorothy, throws the cab-stealer onto the street remarking, "It's incredible how men treat women in this city!" Yet Michael, as himself, is caught in the act of admiring Sandy's feminine wardrobe, and sleeps with Sandy to avoid revealing that he was hired for the acting role that Sandy lost for not being tough enough.

THE FUGITIVE As Dr. Kimble and other prisoners are transported to a state prison, one of the hardened criminals fakes epilepsy as part of an escape plan that ultimately crashes the transport van. Kimble escapes, but true to his decency of character and generosity of spirit, he liberates another lifer from chains, with the reminder to "Be good." U.S. Deputy Marshal Sam Gerard (Tommy Lee Jones) abruptly enters the story, supersedes jurisdiction over the Chicago police, with express orders to serve justice by bringing in Kimble.

Sequence 3 In classic storytelling terms, the protagonist is reluctant to accept the mission: The secret here is that the *reluctance reveals the main* *character's flaw to the audience, but not necessarily to himself.* In the context of the protagonist's newly revealed vulnerability, the storyteller then introduces the *story complication.* Caution, storytellers: This is more than a plot point! The story complication is a story point that reflects itself throughout the entire story: 1) it opposes the dramatic situation, 2) it contradicts the story concept, and 3) it platforms the protagonist's moral choice. It also gives momentum to the story, and necessitates introducing a new character who reflects the protagonist's vulnerability and featured character flaw. This new character, who usually reflects the theme, assists the protagonist in making the difficult moral choice within the story, which the audience hopes is to accept the difficult path presented by the mission. This decision forces the protagonist to overcome internal conflict, embrace the difficult moral conflict, accept the goal or mission of the story, and enter the world where the story takes place.

....

The story complication declares the moral dilemma
with absolute clarity.

....

TITANIC Jack impertinently asks Rose if she loves Cal, and joins Rose, her mother, and Cal for dinner. Molly Brown helps dress and coach Jack, as he enters the rarefied world of the Astors and Guggenheims. Although Jack is treated rudely by Cal because of their class differences, Jack rises to the occasion and distinguishes himself in Rose's eyes. Jack exits, leaving a note inviting Rose to meet him at the clock at the stairs.

TOOTSIE Dorothy shares a dressing room with an actress named April (Geena Davis), and meets Julie Nichols (Jessica Lange), a single mother who plays a nurse on *Southwest General.* Michael also meets the men in Julie's life, including her boyfriend Ron (Dabney Coleman), who's a television director, and her widower father, Les (Charles Durning). Michael puts off Sandy and is permanently annoyed by Ron, the soap opera director who nicknames her "Tootsie," but Dorothy serves her own style of masculine feminism by winning the admiration of her fellow actresses when she refuses to French-kiss fellow actor Dr. Brewster (George Gaynes), and admonishes him to start thinking of her as a person.

THE FUGITIVE Gerard traces Kimble to sewage tunnels, which lead to a dramatic precipice with a waterfall. As they confront each other, Kimble points a gun at Gerard, and rather than pull the trigger, asserts his innocence, "I did not kill my wife." Gerard, who half-believes him for a split second, retorts enigmatically, "I don't care." Lurking inside that magical moment, Gerard is mystified by the fact that Kimble refuses to pull the trigger. By sparing the life of his would-be captor, Kimble makes a moral decision that confounds Gerard, and leaps into the waterfall and becomes a fugitive from injustice. Gerard is fascinated by Kimble's moral strength, but renews his own determination to bring Kimble in.

Act II

Sequence 4 The protagonist enters the world where the story takes place. This world can be a state of mind, a fictional place, an historical event, or a compelling contemporary world we have never seen before. Filled with enthusiasm for the goal or mission, confronting obstacles, tests, allies, and enemies, the protagonist experiences the first setback.

TITANIC Jack invites Rose into third-class steerage, where she dances passionately with Jack and his friends. Later, they experience the promise of romantic love as Jack sketches an erotic portrait of Rose, and that night they consummate their love for one another.

TOOTSIE Dorothy sees Ron kissing April on the set, and Julie asks Dorothy to come over for dinner and help her rehearse her lines. Michael sees this as his "first date" with Julie, and as Dorothy, he presses Julie about why she drinks so much and lets Ron take her for granted. Julie says that just for once she wishes a man would forget the role-playing and just come out and say he'd like to make love. Dorothy, who suddenly realizes (Michael) has stood up Sandy for dinner, leaves in a hurry.

THE FUGITIVE Kimble sets out to find the one-armed man he believes is his wife's killer, changes his appearance, but takes the time to help paramedics diagnose the injury of the prison guard whose gastric tube was punctured during the prisoner escape. Gerard gets his first lead; his team surrounds a false suspect who is killed; and Gerard inadvertently damages the hearing of one of his trusted allies. Gerard coldly states that he refuses to bargain. By his tone, we are certain he means he will not bargain with any man—including his own men—and especially Dr. Richard Kimble!

Sequence 5 The antagonist takes control of the mission with a powerful opposing story thrust, the stakes are raised, and the protagonist falters. Most screenplays fail in sequence 5, (approximately pages 40–50) because the storyteller has not properly constructed the moral dilemma, story complication, and/or the opposing force of the antagonist, and there is not enough conflict to create the thrust of an opposing story that gives momentum within the story.

TITANIC The next morning, Rose's mother disciplines Rose, and presses her to marry Cal for his money. Cal gives an ultimatum to Rose, and sets a plan in motion to falsely set up Jack as a thief and have him arrested. The *Titanic* crew gets news of a weather problem, the warning of an iceberg ahead, and the architect, Mr. Andrews, acknowledges that there are not enough lifeboats for all the passengers aboard the ship.

TOOTSIE Michael arrives three hours late for his dinner date with Sandy. She confronts him with the fact she saw a woman—Michael as Dorothy—enter Michael's apartment, but ends up buying Michael's false excuses, and criticizing Emily Kimberly's performance, suggesting Emily should write her own lines. Michael as Dorothy, irritated by Julie's boyfriend, Ron, and the *Southwest General* French-kissing co-star Dr. Brewster (George Gaynes), begins to rewrite Emily's lines. As Emily comes to the defense of a battered woman, she wins the respect and admiration of Julie; and when Emily introduces a cattle prod to zap Dr. Brewster's "patooties" to keep him in line, television ratings spike upwards.

THE FUGITIVE Dr. Kimble contacts his lawyer, who is legally and ethically unable to help him; and Gerard discovers Kimble is in Chicago. Kimble waits for Dr. Charles Nichols (Jeroen Krabbe), who unbeknownst to Kimble is the villain, outside his tennis club to ask for some money. Nichols gladly helps out Kimble, who takes a basement apartment with a Polish family.

Sequence 6 The protagonist plans to outwit the antagonist and seeks to confront the antagonist on the antagonist's ground. This counterpunch progresses to the midpoint wherein the storyteller revisits the opening premise and images and reiterates the protagonist's mission, only this time, ceding ground to the antagonist, unconsciously informing the audience that the stakes are higher and the moral struggle is even more difficult.

TITANIC One hundred-and-one-year-old Rose, still carrying the heart-shaped blue diamond, continues the story of what happened on the *Titanic* to the present-day exploration crew: The story of the iceberg isn't nearly as interesting as Rose's romance with Jack. Although Jack has ten dollars and nothing to offer Rose but love, dreams, and adventure, Rose, just before the *Titanic* hits the iceberg, decides to cast her lot with Jack, whom Cal has falsely set up as the thief of the blue diamond.

TOOTSIE Julie's father, Les, along with the rest of America, starts to admire Dorothy for her strength of character, and Dorothy begins to appear on the cover of major magazines, creating a national sensation. Julie starts to break from Ron and invites Dorothy to join her and Les at the family farm. Jeff (Bill Murray), Michael's roommate, warns Michael not to go to the farm with Julie, but Michael is determined to be with Julie, insisting that he doesn't owe anything to Sandy because he never told Sandy he loved her, he never promised Sandy he wouldn't see other women, and he didn't tell her about Julie because he didn't want to hurt her feelings.

THE FUGITIVE The Chicago Police return to the case, and Kimble begins to track down the one-armed man through the Cook County General prosthetics department. Gerard questions the villain Dr. Nichols, who alerts them that Kimble is too smart for them. Gerard also questions female doctors who know Kimble well, including one who admits she would have helped him, too. Gerard begins to have doubts about Kimble's guilt, as Kimble breaks into hospital computers to track down all the one-armed men in Chicago. Meanwhile, the son of the Polish family is arrested for drug dealing and tells the police that Kimble is living at their house.

Sequence 7 Faced with the risk of higher stakes, the protagonist struggles against the antagonist, and turns over the first point of control of the mission to the antagonist. This is the first moment of the story when the protagonist senses the possibility of failure. By confronting an adversary who is highly motivated and driven to defeat him, the protagonist experiences a major concession, which shapes his confidence to face the moral dilemma.

TITANIC After the *Titanic* hits an iceberg, Mr. Andrews advises Captain Smith that the ship will go down in two hours and forty minutes. He orders Rose to get into a rescue boat, and life rafts are distributed. Cal asks if there is room for himself, and is told that the rescue boats are only for women and children. With over two thousand souls at risk, Rose refuses to go with her mother; she stays to find Jack and help him rescue the third-class passengers.

TOOTSIE Julie's father teaches Dorothy about courtship and love, as he falls in love with Dorothy's good character and kind nature. Meanwhile, Michael, as Dorothy, falls in love with Julie, who shares her bed with Dorothy and tenderly confides that she (Julie) has spent her entire life hoping for the rosebuds on the wallpaper of her bedroom to bloom. Michael touches Julie, knowing he can give her what she needs, but it means changing his life and ways. He turns over, his wig twists, and for the first time, he realizes the depth of his moral challenge.

THE FUGITIVE Kimble saves the life of a child, and tracks the one-armed man to a false lead at County lock-up, where Gerard hunts him down. After a stairwell chase and a shoot-out, Kimble evades Gerard by slipping into Chicago's St. Patrick's Day Parade, and Gerard, who is beginning to suspect that Kimble may be innocent, issues a "no comment" statement at a press conference, remaining focused on the prize.

Sequence 8 The antagonist takes control of the story now, this time kicking the external struggle into high gear. The protagonist, through his own flaw(s), is fully enmeshed in the territory/world/web of the antagonist, almost ready to surrender to defeat.

TITANIC Rose wades through water looking for Jack who has been handcuffed in a third-class compartment. Without a key, she uses an axe to release him, but the *Titanic* crew has locked them behind a gate, along with hundreds of other third-class passengers. Cal, meanwhile, is on deck "making his own luck" by bribing an official for a place on one of the rescue boats. Jack and his friends crash through the third-class gate, freeing Rose and the other third-class passengers.

TOOTSIE Dorothy receives chocolates from Les; and Dorothy's contract to stay on *Southwest General* for a second season is renewed, which means Michael is locked into playing Emily. As Julie begins to resist Ron, Ron confronts Dorothy about why Dorothy doesn't like him. Ron defends his behavior by telling Dorothy that he never told Julie he loved her, he never promised he'd be exclusive to her, and that he knows Julie doesn't want him to see other women, but he lies to her keep from hurting her feelings. Michael, as Dorothy, begins to see himself through Tootsie's eyes.

THE FUGITIVE Kimble tracks the one-armed man, a former cop named Sykes (Andreas Katsulas), to an apartment, discovering photos of Sykes with one of Kimble's colleagues, Dr. Lentz (David Darlow). Kimble remembers surgically treating a patient for hemorrhaging who had been using the newly approved wonder drug Provasic and subsequently died of liver damage. Kimble calls Gerard from the apartment, leading him to a big piece of the puzzle. Sykes arrives home as Gerard and his team realize Sykes is "dirty"; and Kimble naively contacts Nichols, announcing he's found the one-armed man who murdered his wife. Nichols tells Kimble that Lentz is dead.

Sequence 9 The antagonist defeats the protagonist, both physically and morally, and the protagonist loses his motivation, direction, and temporarily turns his back on the mission.

TITANIC The ship's steward tries to keep order, as Cal orders Rose to get on the boat, telling her he's made arrangements for Jack and himself. When Rose complies, Jack confronts Cal, who admits that there is no arrangement for Jack. Rose escapes from the rescue boat back to the *Titanic,* to be with Jack. Cal tries to kill Jack. Jack escapes with Rose, who is wearing Jack's coat with the blue heart-shaped diamond.

TOOTSIE Dorothy survives baby-sitting Julie's daughter Amy (Amy Lawrence), and feelings begin to develop between Dorothy and Julie, who mistakes Dorothy's attachment as lesbian in nature. Les invites Dorothy on a date and presents her with a diamond engagement ring and a proposal of marriage. Dorothy abruptly exits for home, only to find soap opera co-star Dr. Brewster professing his romantic affections for her as well. Sandy shows up unexpectedly, and when Michael tries to make amends by giving her the chocolates with the love note from Les, Sandy concludes that Michael is gay. Michael finally admits he is in love with another woman.

THE FUGITIVE Gerard tracks down the villain, Dr. Nichols, who claims he doesn't know Lentz. Kimble tracks the liver samples used in the drug trials, discovers they were false, and Gerard confirms that Nichols lied about knowing Lentz. Kimble is pursued and attacked on the subway by Sykes, the one-armed man, who kills a Chicago policeman in the fracas, and Kimble escapes, once again a fugitive on the run, but this time thought to be a cop killer.

Act III

Sequence 10 The protagonist surrenders his mission and relinquishes his motivation, but resurrects his moral direction by confronting his personal flaw. By recovering moral strength, the protagonist reinstates the mission, once again driving him forward. He achieves enough success to keep us on the edge of our seats, only to be defeated again, this time experiencing a devastating setback, one that casts doubt as to whether he will ever achieve his mission, despite his moral growth.

TITANIC Jack and Rose try to rescue a child in third class, as Cal steals a child to get a seat on one of the rescue boats. The steward, who is trying to keep order, kills a man who tries to get on the boat, and then turns the gun on himself. Mr. Andrews, the architect, gives Rose a life vest, and Mr. Guggenheim (Michael Ensign) prepares to go down like a gentleman, drinking a brandy, as the musicians play. The captain refuses to leave the bridge, as Cal pushes someone off a rescue boat to make room for himself and the child he has kidnapped. The child Jack and Rose tried to rescue goes underwater, and so do Jack and Rose.

TOOTSIE Michael demands that his agent George (Sydney Pollack) get him out of the contract and off the show, but George warns him they could be sued for fraud. The cast and crew of *Southwest General* prepare for a live broadcast of Emily's party scene, as Dorothy tries to make amends with Julie by bringing a gift for Amy. Julie kindly tells Dorothy that she loves her, but can't truly love her.

THE FUGITIVE Dr. Nichols addresses a medical convention at a hotel, promoting the newly approved wonder drug Provasic. Kimble goads him off the stage, publicly revealing how deadly Provasic can be, while Gerard is hot on their trail. Kimble nearly defeats Nichols in the hotel kitchen, but they both free-fall down the service elevator to the laundry floor.

Sequence 11 The protagonist rises again, this time marshaling both his moral strength and external forces to face the antagonist. However, before they confront each other on-screen in a face-to-face conflict, the protagonist experiences a deep personal understanding pertaining to his/her internal struggle. This important moment—the moment of realization, or epiphany—is what the audience has been waiting for. It occurs just before the climax and satisfies the audience on two levels: It reveals the protagonist's personal insight and resolution of his or her character flaw; and it provides a greater understanding of the moral accomplishment of the mission and how this reflects itself as a greater understanding of humanity.

TITANIC As the ship goes down, the priest blesses the souls of the lost passengers. The irrepressible Molly Brown (Kathy Bates) insists that the passengers of her rescue boat transfer to another, sending their rescue boat back to save a few more. Jack and Rose, meanwhile, plunge into the freezing water, and Jack helps Rose onto a floating bed board, with the promise not to let go. As Molly Brown's boat makes its way through frozen, dead bodies, looking for signs of life, Rose makes her way to a dead crewman wearing a whistle, and is rescued. Jack has died in the night.

TOOTSIE During the live broadcast, Dorothy concocts Emily Kimberly's over-the-top back-story, announcing that she is actually Emily's brother, Edward Kimberly, and that he has returned to *Southwest General* to settle a score. As everyone reacts, Michael rips off his disguise, piece-by-piece, and announces that he was "strong enough to be a woman, which was the best part of my manhood."

THE FUGITIVE Kimble rises from the service elevator, now in the laundry room, and so does Nichols. Gerard appears, warning Kimble that he knows what happened, that he knows who's behind the murders, and that it's time to give up. Before Kimble gives up, Nichols appears from around a corner, with his gun aimed at Gerard. Kimble attacks Nichols, stopping Nichols from shooting Gerard.

Sequence 12 His mission complete, the protagonist returns home where the story began, but with the internal satisfaction of nurturing a deeply valued treasure pertaining to a more meaningful life, whether it is a loved one, an ideal, or wisdom, victory, or peace.

TITANIC Fifteen hundred died, and out of twenty boats, only Molly's came back to look for more to rescue. Molly saved six people: seven hundred survivors on the other nineteen boats waited for absolution that would never come. Cal lost everything in 1929 and killed himself, and although there is no record of Jack, 101-year-old Rose makes the realization that Jack "saved me in every way a person can be saved" allowing her to live life bigger for having known him. After Rose throws the heart-shaped blue diamond back to the sea, she sees young Jack at the top of the stairs of the *Titanic,* and dreams of their ultimate union with the memory of a romantic kiss.

TOOTSIE Michael apologizes to Les and returns the ring. After some time has passed, he waits for Julie as she exits the studio. She's reticent about seeing Michael because he's broken her trust, but mentions she misses Dorothy. Michael says she doesn't have to miss Dorothy, because she's right here in him: "I was a better man with you as a woman than I was as a man with a woman." Unable to convince Julie that he is worthy of her, Michael suggests that there might be an advantage to his wearing pants at this stage of their relationship. Julie, who is almost convinced, takes it slowly, suggesting she may be willing to give him a try by humorously testing him with the ultimate girlfriend-to-girlfriend favor, "Will you loan me that pretty yellow outfit?"

THE FUGITIVE At a news conference, the Chicago police deliver Sykes, the one-armed man. Gerard escorts Kimble into custody, uncuffs him and offers him an ice pack. Kimble remarks Gerard's brief act of humanity, "Thought you didn't care." "I don't," answers Gerard. "Don't tell anybody."

ADVANCED 3-ACT, 12-SEQUENCE STORY FORM

3-6-3 Sequence Form

Act I	Act II	Act III
Seq. 1, 2, 3	Seq. 4, 5, 6, 7, 8, 9	Seq. 10, 11, 12

Paradigms are archetypes, or examples, that are clear. This Advanced 3-Act, 12-Sequence Story Form can be broken down into 3-6-3 sequence form, with three sequences in act one, six sequences in act two, and three sequences in act three. It provides the framework through which we can visualize the invisible structure of the story, which is filled with spontaneous moments of human behavior. This form also provides the guidelines and checklist from which we can see what is missing in our stories as we are floundering about with the plot, discovering what the story is about, listening to our unconscious, and creating characters that reflect the ideas that convey the deeper meaning of the story.

Most screenwriters believe in form—not secret formulas—but that doesn't stop us from pursuing the possibility that one exists, and is yet to be discovered. Just like the great Ben Hogan golf swing that can be mastered by learning the fundamentals—but may difficult to repeat, the secret formula of screenwriting is within the grasp of most screenwriters, but requires years of practice. It is a combination of fundamentals, form, paradigms, technique, timing, originality, tone, and individual expression, supported by the process of storytelling.

CHAPTER SIX

Spine: The Process

ONE of the most difficult points to understand about the process of storytelling is that there are *ideas behind the story*. Most writers are so anxious to get started with *what they think is screenwriting*, they forget that they are telling a story that reflects deep and personal ideas, and instead, they dedicate their energies to connecting the dots of a plot structured in the basic 3-Act Paradigm. Then they launch full-throttle into scene-writing, complete with characters and dialogue, without taking the time to think about what their story is about, let alone considering the thematic possibilities and opportunities within their story. Consequently, they inhibit their artistic and professional growth, never tapping into their genius and unique voice to enhance the storytelling process.

IDEAS BEHIND THE STORY

The ideas behind the story become the story. In fact, these abstract ideas—what your story is about—transform into characters and behavior throughout the story, negating and supporting each other, revealing complex ideas about the main character and universal truths about the human condition. Sophisticated screenwriters call the unity of this process the *spine of the story.*

Spine is the dynamic idea that guides the story.
We derive behavior from spine.

Be prepared to struggle to understand spine. Be prepared to be frustrated. Be prepared to fail. Although the struggle can bring great rewards, very few screenwriters successfully create spine because it is difficult to understand, let alone to break it down into a process that can be mastered. Tennessee Williams did it by instinct. So did Jason Miller. I learned spine by osmosis from working with them, and gradually integrated the dynamics of this mysterious process into a primitive model, using ideas behind the story as characters that create conflict. Later, I studied film scripts and films, especially the work of Stephen Zaillian (*Searching for Bobby Fischer, Schindler's List*), James Cameron (*Titanic, The Abyss, Terminator*), and Sydney Pollack (*Out of Africa, Tootsie, The Way We Were*). Pollack credits the Stanislavski method as the basis for this system, but for me, early educational references to nineteenth-century German philosopher Georg Hegel shaped my understanding of the storytelling process. Hegel's system, which is detailed later, describes a process that juxtaposes opposing and contradictory ideas to resolve conflict.

In storytelling, ideas become characters, constantly in conflict,
until the resolution.

Observing that great writers work unconsciously—as problem solvers—I was able to break down the storytelling process for myself, and later for others, in problem-solving terms. Again, keep in mind that all writers struggle with developing effective spine, but it can be learned by a combination of experience and example, so take your time until the process feels comfortable.

ESTABLISH THEME TO CREATE SPINE

Spine begins with establishing an idea, or *theme,* that conveys what the story is about. But spine is more than theme; it is a process of distilling the ideas behind the story, and reducing the ideas into a dynamic principle, from which we can derive behavior.

Without the spine of the story, the screenplay is merely a series of scenes or set of events that, in fact, may not express a story idea or plot, let alone be a movie script. This does not mean you should abandon your ideas and plots that have not been properly conceived and developed with a spine; it just means that you are going to have to give yourself over to the process of establishing a theme within the premise, creating ideas behind the story, and *morphing ideas into characters and behavior.* Once you begin to understand the layers to this process, you can teach yourself to re-think your work and re-conceive your story ideas in a professional way.

How Does Spine Differ from Theme?

Theme is a dialectic idea that is the *basis of the story premise.* Spine is a dynamic idea, or principle, which emerges from the moral dilemma of the story. Spine represents the transformation of the main character and reveals the depth of the story.

Theme

Theme is the preliminary understanding of *what the story is about.* It is an intellectual notion or an abstract idea. For story purposes, you might explore theme by asking a question that moves the process forward. For example, if you begin with the idea of "trust and betrayal," you might transform it into a storyline by asking "What if your life depended upon trusting a human being who betrayed you?" An example of a question to help develop the theme of "love and need" might be: "What if you were faced with the choice of saving only one of your two children: the child who loves you or the child who needs you?" Let's look at three contemporary examples:

TITANIC What if you, along with thousands of others, faced a major disaster and imminent death? Would you save yourself or risk your life to save others?

TOOTSIE What if you were a desperate, out-of-work, actor whose last job was playing a tomato? Would you put on a skirt to get a job even if it meant you had to change everything about your life, including your lifestyle and attitude toward women?

THE FUGITIVE What if you were sentenced to death for a murder you did not commit? Would you run from injustice without regard for others, or would you use your wits to hunt down the real murderer and bring him to justice? More important, while doing so, would you exercise your humanity and save the lives of others if necessary?

Storytellers begin with theme as a basis for the story premise, and through the process of negating the idea—creating a dialectic—gradually discover the ideas behind the story. These ideas emerge as characters, and their behavior becomes the basis for the spine.

....

Theme is the idea that becomes the basis for the story.
Negating the theme leads to the ideas behind the story.
Theme = What the story is about.

....

Ideas behind the story convey a larger concept—a group of ideas—that grows out of negating the theme. They are life-affirming concepts that support the struggle of the human condition. As the storyteller comes to understand the depth of these ideas, the storyteller transforms these ideas into characters and behavior, always through conflict, creating paradoxes and contradictions, negating and supporting one another throughout the story. The cumulative effect of character–driven conflict forms the *spine* of the story.

When spine is working *as behavior* through conflict, it becomes *dynamic and human,* revealing itself throughout each and every scene. The audience emotionally attaches to the spine through the main character in order to understand the evolving ideas behind the story, which fade as the main character confronts his foibles and adversaries along the way. At the end of the story, the main character makes a mature personal understanding of what he has accomplished, and this realization reveals the comprehensive truth, or universal truth, which we refer to as the moral of the story.

The ideas behind the story are inextricably linked to the *world where the story takes place.* This may seem fundamental, but quite often writers create a movie without establishing a fascinating world where the story takes place. Still others create an interesting world and then shortchange their exciting locale by creating a mediocre story. Great movies make use of both:

TITANIC The world of this movie, the "unsinkable" R.M.S. *Titanic,* is where fate thrusts on its passengers the morally compelling choice to save themselves or risk their lives to save those around them.

TOOTSIE The world of femininity and women's lib is where a self-serving, narcissistic out-of-work actor learns what it means to be a better man when he poses as a woman by winning the role of a feisty gal nicknamed "Tootsie."

THE FUGITIVE The world of a fugitive from injustice is where Dr. Richard Kimble (Harrison Ford), an honorable man, is forced to break the law in order to prove his innocence, as he hunts down the one-armed man who murdered his wife.

Ideas behind the story are *abstract,* meaning the story expresses qualities and ideas that reflect more than the characters, scenes, and plot suggest. These ideas can be difficult to understand because they are disassociated from any specific instance in the story. In other words, the events of the story are concrete, but they suggest powerful ideas that the audience infers cumulatively and unconsciously.

TITANIC Would you sacrifice your life for the one you love?

TOOTSIE Is it possible to love another human being without putting aside our selfish ways?

THE FUGITIVE How do we become worthy of mercy, in the face of injustice?

Ideas behind the story are different from *subtext.* Subtext is the underlying meaning behind the action, scenes, and dialogue. It's what we infer directly from the material, and what we consciously interpret from how the characters make us feel. The audience might easily understand the subtext of a scene or sequence but struggle to comprehend the *ideas behind the story* as these abstract ideas unfold slowly and develop in sequences with opposing forces within the characters and dialogue.

TITANIC Jack is willing to risk his life for Rose the moment he meets her. When he risks his life for others and gives up his life for her, he inspires Rose's affection and eternal love.

TOOTSIE Michael puts aside his selfish, womanizing ways when he sees himself through the eyes of Tootsie.

THE FUGITIVE Dr. Richard Kimble not only did not kill his wife; he is an extra-ordinary man whose goodness of character inspires those around him, espe-cially the man who doggedly pursues him.

Spine = Process

Because developing spine requires working with intuition in the ab-stract world, it holds a great deal of mystique for screenwriters and di-rectors. Although best learned from experience, spine can be understood as a process, and mastered one script at a time.

> Spine is the guiding principle from which we derive
> human behavior.
> Using spine, we develop characters and behavior.
> Spine reveals the depth of the story.

The genius behind a great screenplay is to know how to persevere with the ideas behind the story until the story reveals a *universal truth*. Truth means a judgment, proposition, or an idea that we as human be-ings hold to be factual and real. The standards for "universal truth" are even more rigorous, because lurking inside the spiritual world of uni-versal truth there are transcendent fundamentals, principles, or ideals that speak to all human beings, regardless of culture.

The process of creating spine can be broken down into eight essen-tial steps. Keep in mind that this is a description of a *process,* not a for-mula. The process is creative and dynamic, which means all steps are necessary, but they are achieved cumulatively, sometimes concurrently, sometimes one at a time. The ability to create spine—through charac-ters and behavior—is the hallmark of an A-list screenplay.

CREATING SPINE IN THE A-LIST SCREENPLAY

Define the story premise.
Establish theme.
Morph thematic ideas into characters.
Define the action of the story: Plot.
Define the underlying action of the story: subtext.

MOST SCREENWRITERS STOP HERE.

Discover the ideas behind the story.
Create the spine of the story.
Using spine, morph ideas back into the story as
characters and behavior.

As you study the following examples, keep in mind that these are merely steps and descriptions meant to introduce you to the process. It is much easier to describe spine by example than to create spine within a story.

Titanic Jack Dawson wins a third class ticket to America on the R.M.S. *Titanic* where he falls in love with Rose DeWitt, whose cash-poor upper-class mother is determined to see her daughter marry Cal Hockley, a narcissistic wealthy cad. Jack and Rose's love can never be, however, not because of class differences, rather because of the fate of the "unsinkable" *Titanic,* which is introduced to the audience as "The Ship of Dreams." Jack, who is willing to give up his life for Rose, wins her enduring love. Rose, at the end of her life, freely gives the beautiful heart-shaped blue diamond back to *Titanic,* and in so doing, expresses her last wish to be reunited with Jack for eternity.

The subtext of *Titanic* is that Jack, a true hero, is willing to give up his life for others, even though he dreams of a fulfilling life for himself in America with the woman he loves. We are not absolutely certain of this based on factual presentation, but because of the movie's subtext, we are emotionally convinced that because of Jack's extraordinary talent, he could win Rose's hand in marriage and provide a fulfilling life for her in America, a place where the content of one's character matters most and one's class does not interfere with one's ability to pursue happiness. Conversely, Cal Hockley opposes Jack for Rose's affections, arousing our deepest suspicions, especially with regard to Rose's happiness. In fact, we are emotionally convinced that he is unworthy of Rose, and we are morally repulsed by his condescending, egocentric behavior, especially when he abducts a baby and masquerades as a father to usurp a seat on one of the rescue boats.

The subtext is clear to everyone who sees the movie, without much dramatic explanation. However, it's the subtext of the story that leads us down the pathway into the ideas behind the story, which are otherwise abstract: Would you be willing to sacrifice your life for the one you love?

Titanic is about the inevitability of death in the face of human disaster, where in one final moment, each human being has the opportunity to make the ultimate life choice, that is, choosing between personal self-interests or the willingness to sacrifice one's life for others. In this story based on a true-life historical event, there were actually two hours and forty minutes from the moment of collision with the iceberg until the ship flooded, spiked, and eventually went down. What makes the story compelling, however, is that without explicit reference to eternity or mention of the possibility of the afterlife, *Titanic,* the Ship of Dreams, holds great fascination as a metaphor for how we value life, which is finite. The romantics among us recognize that while there are classes that divide us, our humanity can rise above class distinctions; Jack and Rose's love proves that. For others, such as the shipbuilder Mr. Andrews, the *Titanic* represents the false pride of humanity. For Captain Smith, who holds onto the wheel until the ship goes down, the *Titanic* represents one last chance to save humanity from its collision course with Fate. For Jacob Astor, it represents honor over self-preservation. For the crewmen who load the rescue boats and assist passengers into safety, it represents duty over self-preservation. For the priest who blesses the doomed souls that surround him, it represents a chance to save his own soul by saving others. For the unsinkable Molly Brown (Kathy Bates) who is lucky enough to get a spot on one of the life boats, the events of that night represent a chance to risk her own life to save one more human being. *Titanic* struck a chord for millions of moviegoers—$2 billion worldwide worth—ultimately, however, the story has great impact on us because we identify with Jack's selfless act to give up his life for others, as well as his faith and hope that he will be reunited with Rose for eternity. His act of heroism stirs our hope, that we, too, are capable of selflessness and enduring love, and that if we trust destiny as Rose does, we will experience the greatest gift of all, to be reunited with our loved ones for eternity.

WHAT IS THE SPINE OF *TITANIC*? By the selfless act of giving up his life for others, Jack wins the enduring love of Rose, and is blessed with the hope of reuniting with her for eternity.

Poignant, memorable moments build throughout the piece as each character faces his or her moment of destiny. The final moment of genius occurs when Rose, in contemplation of her own death, gives the heart-shaped diamond back to *Titanic* and in so doing, expresses her deepest wish to be reunited with Jack. As the image of young Jack fills the screen, we feel the sense of enduring love, together with a mature woman's romantic dream that they will come together again, for all eternity. In that moment that she releases her diamond back to *Titanic* we experience the depth of a life journey that is universal and complete.

Tootsie Michael Dorsey is a narcissistic, out-of-work actor who was fired from his last job—playing a tomato. He's also a womanizer who takes his actress girlfriend, Sandy, for granted. In fact, his life is a mess; no one will hire him; and the only way out of his misery is to put on a skirt and audition for a soap opera role as hospital administrator to Emily Kimberly, an acting job Sandy wanted. Michael wins the role dressed as a woman named Dorothy Michaels, and develops a friendship with his co-star Julie (Jessica Lange) who portrays a nurse on the show. Unbeknownst to Julie, Michael becomes romantically interested in her off-screen, even though she is involved with the show's director,

Ron, (Dabney Coleman), a hopeless womanizer who nicknames Dorothy "Tootsie." Michael, as Dorothy, stands up to Ron, befriends Julie, becomes a national icon, and attracts the admiration of Julie's widower father (Charles Durning). His experiences as Dorothy and his friendship with Julie enable him to see himself through Tootsie's eyes, and he doesn't like what he sees. In order to restore his self-respect and win the love and admiration of Julie, Michael is forced to confront the truth about himself.

The subtext of the story is clear: Michael is a selfish man, unworthy of any woman. In fact, for Michael to win back his self-worth and the affections of Julie, he must make some serious changes in his life, but it's not until he attracts the romantic interest of Julie's father that he realizes what it means to be loyal, loving, and gentlemanly. Moreover, it's not until he sees the same false motives and personal flaws in Ron that he realizes what an awful cad he's been.

Tootsie is about becoming a better man. Although he helps Sandy prepare for the audition, he takes her for granted and deceives her by auditioning for the role himself. As Dorothy, Michael gets his first dose of chauvinism at the audition, but it's the rude man who beats Dorothy out of a taxicab that opens the key to the story. Dorothy literally tosses him out of the taxi and onto the street, beating him with shopping bags. Later, Dorothy objects to Ron nicknaming her "Tootsie" and slaps fellow soap actor Dr. Brewster (George Gaynes) for his French kiss attempt on Dorothy. Michael and Dorothy start to merge together psychologically, however, when Dorothy catches Julie's boyfriend, Ron, kissing Julie's friend April (Geena Davis) on the set. The story twist pays off later when Julie confides to Dorothy that, for just once, she would like a man to approach her with a simple line like, "Listen, I could lay a big line on you, and we could do a lot of role playing, but the simple truth is that I would really like to make love to you." However, when Michael casually approaches Julie at a party using her preferred pick-up line, she dumps a glass of wine on him. Another contradiction occurs when Michael deceives Sandy and defends his caddish behavior to his roommate (Bill Murray), only to hear his rationale repeated by his archnemesis Ron pertaining to Julie: "I never told Julie that we were exclusive.

I never told her that I wouldn't see other women. I didn't want to tell her because I didn't want to hurt her feelings. I didn't want to tell her to protect her." Michael, as Dorothy, quips, "I understand you better than you think I do." In fact, at this moment, Michael understands himself for the first time through "Tootsie," creating a platform—a story point with absolute clarity—that highlights what the story is really about.

WHAT IS THE SPINE OF *TOOTSIE?* By becoming a woman, Michael becomes a better man. From the moment Dorothy kicks the man out of the taxicab, to the moment when Julie tosses the glass of wine into Michael's face to the point when Michael makes the final realization that he has a lot to learn about becoming a better man, we see ourselves, *not as men and women playing roles with each other,* but as human beings struggling with letting go of our own egotistic needs and desires. The final touch of genius, however, graces the end of the story: Michael approaches Julie with the hope that they can have a romantic relationship. Julie is skeptical, but Michael reminds her that they have already worked through the hard part and at this point, there might be an advantage to his wearing pants. Julie, who is almost convinced, humorously appeals to the Dorothy inside Michael—the generous, caring side—suggesting she is willing to give it a try: "Will you loan me that pretty yellow outfit?" Michael, who is determined to shed his old ways to win Julie's heart, mock-resists letting go of the yellow Halston, but ultimately concedes, and with that, the story is complete.

The Fugitive Dr. Richard Kimble is falsely accused and convicted of killing his wife. He flees, not from justice, *but from injustice,* and is a man on the run in search of the one-armed man who murdered his wife. Dr. Kimble is not an ordinary man; he is a man of integrity with good moral character. He is a do-gooder up against *blind justice,* which, in this case, is unjust, as represented by Officer Sam Gerard (Tommy Lee Jones).

The subtext of the piece is that Dr. Kimble is an innocent man who is condemned to death for a crime he did not commit. Of course, we are not absolutely certain of Kimble's innocence based on factual presentation; however, *because of the subtext of the movie,* we are emotionally convinced, from the very beginning, that Dr. Kimble loved his wife and would never have murdered her. Conversely, as Officer Gerard enters the story, we are suspicious of Gerard's motive to bring Kimble to justice, but we are emotionally convinced throughout the story that Officer Gerard believes it is his job to uphold the laws of man, no matter how unjust.

The subtext of the story leads us to understand the ideas behind the story: Kimble is a do-gooder, but not just a simple do-gooder. He is a *fugitive from injustice,* and we, as the audience, have a chance to participate in our own redemption through Gerard and by granting Kimble a reprieve. Kimble inspires strong feelings in all whom he encounters. There are those who love him, admire him, and follow him in awe and appreciation for his love for mankind: the hardened criminal he releases to freedom, the prison escort whose life he saves by diagnosing the gastric puncture, the two female doctors who are his loyal colleagues, the young boy whose life he saves by rewriting his emergency room instructions, and the emergency room doctor (Julianne Moore) who inadvertently raises the momentum of the story by appealing to Gerard's competitive male ego. And yet, there are those who betray Kimble, mock him, and seek to destroy him to advance their own malevolent interests, all under the guise of upholding the laws of man: the one-armed man who is a corrupt cop, the villain Dr. Nichols (Jeroen Krabbe), the ever-present Captain Kelly and the Chicago Police Department who want to claim credit for his capture, and of course, U. S. Marshal Sam Gerard and his team, each of who reflects a different aspect of Gerard's inner conflict. Cosmo (Joe Pantoliano) is practical, overly concerned about ruining his new shoes; all he wants to do is close up the case and go home. His female counterpoint, Poole (L. Scott Caldwell), is the keeper of the facts, skeptical of Gerard, always throwing doubt on his assumptions. Newman (Tom Wood) represents Gerard's conscience, thoughtful and conflicted: He understands the sum total of Dr. Richard Kimble, which ultimately represents the truth, which is why Gerard eventually adopts Newman's perspective. In short, this is a superb action piece, but the story is world class because the ideas behind the story are character-driven, complex, satisfying, and meaningful. Interestingly, although Kimble portrays an epic hero who is a do-gooder, it is Gerard whose story we unconsciously follow, because Gerard experiences the conflict of the moral dilemma to bring in Kimble. As Gerard transforms from within, we identify with his transformation as our own.

WHAT IS THE SPINE OF *THE FUGITIVE*? By effecting goodness among his fellow man, Richard Kimble, the fugitive from injustice, inspires those who falsely condemn him to emulate his behavior.

The first poignant moment of the movie occurs when Kimble is condemned to death by lethal injection by a judge who rules, "May God have mercy on your soul." From that point on, we, as the audience, hope Kimble will win a reprieve, not just for his own sake, but for ourselves, because we identify with the injustice he has suffered. More profoundly, we secretly hope that whatever injustice we may face in our own lives will be met with mercy, not vengeance.

IDEAS AS CHARACTERS

Storytelling requires working with "ideas as characters" from the inside out, establishing what the story is about thematically, morphing these ideas into characters and behavior, defining the subtext as the emotional compass, developing these *ideas behind the story* on multiple levels that feed into one another, and creating the spine of the story where these ideas negate and support each other, while developing the concrete narrative into a story progression. There are many levels to the storytelling process, and discovering how to use characterization to solve story problems is a major step forward.

CHAPTER SEVEN

Integrating Form and Spine

THERE is a temptation for most screenwriters to see form and spine as separate and distinct from one another, which makes screenwriting look deceptively easy.

Form is the invisible 3-Act, 12-sequence structure.
Spine depicts the main character's transformation through a dynamic central idea.

Storytelling in screenplay form, however, is complex. It requires knowing how to integrate these two complementary approaches by synthesizing story elements and structure through the main character's internal transformation. This is called *character-driven story structure*. Integrating form and spine begins with developing a main character whose internal struggle reveals the story. However, before you can fully develop the main character, it is important to understand the interactive process and layers involved with the six stages of storytelling.

SIX STAGES OF STORYTELLING

Stage One: Creating the Main Character Who Drives the Story

Once you have committed to the basic story concept, the challenge is to create a main character *who drives the story*. While you might not know every single detail about the main character before you begin, at the minimum, you must have a sense of who he or she is psychologically, the back-story, and the forward-moving action of the plot, with a sense of what the story is about. This ongoing task requires constant attention, and merits and an entire chapter, "Creating the Main Character" (Chapter Eleven). At this stage, however, as you are working out the more subtle elements of story—moral dilemma, unconscious conflict, and story complication—you prepare the story *through the main character* in order to lay the foundation for other story elements.

Stage Two: Creating Conflict Within the Story

The next challenge is to create *as much conflict as possible for the main character* from the beginning, through the middle, to the end. Creating conflict does not result from creating plots, subplots, and obstacles for the main character to overcome; it comes from defining the internal conflict within the main character and understanding the unconscious drives that motivate him or her. This inner struggle is expressed through other characters who—*in external conflict with the main character*—give the audience a greater understanding of what the story is about.

Create as much conflict as possible for the main character.

Often, a writer will start with an intriguing concept and a few interesting characters but not know how to efficiently express the story through the main character. I have developed many true stories and biographies for dramatic presentation. In biographical material, there is always a main character who has led an interesting life or experienced an incident within his or her life that lends itself to a story. There are also additional true-life characters who serve the story, but inevitably, there are not enough characters to tell the story dramatically, so the writer sometimes has to create fictional supporting characters who represent aspects of the theme or spine that are not addressed in the factual presentation of the story. This is done to enhance the story and the overall transformation of the main character.

Knowing how to create conflict within the story begins with establishing motivation, *so that the audience identifies with the main character.* Creating conflict with supporting characters is the first step to creating a memorable story with impact. Establishing the motivation of the main character is another important task, so much so that it requires creating a platform within the story. Creating a platform means creating a scene or sequence that declares a story point with absolute clarity. In this regard, everyone in the audience immediately understands what's going on inside the main character.

Creating a platform means declaring a story point with
absolute clarity.

Once the platform is established, subtle nuances of characterizations, which are often called "shades," or if they are lacking, "missing shades" of characterization, are revealed through conflict with supporting characters. Sometimes this is achieved unconsciously and intuitively through internal conflict. Other times, it is stated consciously and deliberately through external conflict. Together, both types of conflict create a three-dimensional world filled with lifelike characters who help the audience see the narrative on-screen and, by inference, understand the emotional depth of the story.

Stage Three: Developing Contrast Between and Among the Characters

Just like each and every individual we meet is unique, each and every character developed within a story has his or her own personality and backstory. In storytelling, however, each character functions in relation to the main character and the story goal of the main character. The character-driven story structure develops exponentially, in both positive and negative directions, moving forward to a final, absolute symmetry, culminating in the climax of the story. This dynamic movement of the story, called story progression, occurs when each character contrasts, supports, or negates not only the main character, but one another throughout the story. This occurs consciously for the audience, but there is also an unconscious component, which the audience infers not only through character conflict, but through the use of symbolism, point of view, and tone, which are covered in Chapter Twenty, "Originality."

Story progression is created by the overt interaction between and among the characters, and drives the character-driven story to its conclusion.

I have read many promising screenplays that lack focus because the writer has not developed sufficient or key characters that tell the story. Without vivid, poignant characters who serve to connect, ignite, confront, or otherwise spark the main character's story, an essential piece of the overall story and its conflict is lost.

• Imagine *Titanic* without Molly Brown. She prepares Jack for dinner with Rose, Rose's class-conscious mother (Frances Fisher), and her malevolent fiancé, Cal. In fact, Molly is preparing Jack for his date with destiny and ultimately she reveals herself to be like Jack, risking her own life to rescue others. What would this epic story be like without the proud architect, Mr. Anderson, who believed *Titanic* was unsinkable? There would be no cautionary tale inside the story!

• Imagine *The Fugitive* without Gerard's investigative team, who discover contradictory evidence that exculpates Dr. Kimble, and challenge Gerard psychologically and morally. What would this thought-provoking story be like without Chicago Detective Kelly, who bluffs his way through his own pseudo-investigation, undercutting Gerard to advance his career? Without Kelly, there would be no texture to the story, no formative comparison with Gerard, who serves as the contrast to Dr. Kimble.

• Imagine *Tootsie* without Julie's father, Les. If Les did not fall in love with Michael as Dorothy, there would be no center to the story, nor would there be a counter-romance to Michael's affection for Julie. Without Michael's best friend, Jeff, who helps us understand Michael's struggle to become a better man, there would be no moral compass to challenge Michael's self-serving antics.

Stage Four: Defining Spine by Sequences

Once a writer begins to understand the dynamic of spine and how to use characters to develop the spine within the story, the next step requires a leap of faith. Defining the twelve story points (mini-climaxes) that drive the twelve sequences toward the story climax begins with identifying the major conflict between the main character and the antagonist, and defining twelve points of conflict. For most writers, this is very difficult because it means *creating characters and behavior that reflect the ideas behind the story.* Keep in mind that virtually all story problems and story solutions originate in character development and conflict. It may help you to think of spine as "dramatic argumentation" with many shades and nuances, which are represented by characters. In this analogy, each character represents his or her "dramatic argument" supporting or negating what the story is about.

- In *Titanic,* Cal directly negates Jack in comedic ways. Cal is proud, controlling, envious, spiteful. In the end, he proves himself to be a coward, especially in conflict with Jack for Rose's affection.

- In *Tootsie,* Dorothy negates Michael in comedic ways. Dorothy is forthright, decent, generous, and loyal. In the end, Michael proves himself *to be Dorothy,* especially in conflict with Ron for Julie's affection.

- In *The Fugitive,* Gerard indirectly negates Kimble in ironic ways. Gerard is arrogant, unsympathetic, ruthless, and driven. In the end, Gerard proves himself to be grateful and appreciative, especially in conflict with Kimble who tracks down the one-armed man.

With this in mind, spine reveals itself through characters in conflict, moment by moment, scene by scene, sequence by sequence.

....

Think of spine as "dramatic argumentation."
Each character represents his or her "dramatic argument."
Each "dramatic argument" supports or negates what the
story is about.

....

Stage Five: Building Toward the Climax Using Spine

A story has a beginning, middle, and end. A great story begins with a fascinating character and compelling dramatic situation. Great storytelling requires knowing *how to use ideas as characters* to develop the compelling dramatic situation from the beginning, through the middle of the story, into the climax of the story. One of the subtleties is learning to appreciate that what we experience as *"story"* is the abstract understanding about the *internal conflict of the main character,* as presented in the compelling dramatic situation, challenged throughout Act II, and resolved at the climax.

Keep in mind that the spine doesn't just happen. It requires constant thinking, curiosity, and development. It deepens as you write and rewrite a script, but always at the forefront is the challenge that you must make conscious decisions about theme and spine from the very beginning, so that you can discover opportunities to develop unconscious details and subtle dynamics of the characters as you move along toward the climax.

Stage Six: Revealing the Depth of the Story Through Spine

The "depth of the story" is what we feel about the story in our hearts; this is how we experience the story emotionally, intellectually. If you have established the foundation of the story by creating spine, depicting characters that reveal spine, using spine to discover what is missing from the story, and developing characters and behavior that become spine, you are on the path of revealing the depth of the story. Your audience will experience the story emotionally through the main character, moment by moment, scene by scene, sequence by sequence, to its final conclusion.

The Story Paradox

An interesting paradox emerges at this stage of storytelling. Although you may tell a story moment by moment, and the audience feels you are telling the story moment by moment, storytellers actually reveal the story with a comprehensive overview of all the ideas behind the story. In fact, the only way to tell a story with emotional depth is to become alert to its mysteries from the very beginning, recognizing that you will spontaneously discover insights about your characters and story as you move along. Then, as you work in sequences, you will find yourself creating even more story layers than you could ever imagine! This process is merciless, and it is never-ending, so prepare for the fact that there is an infinite depth to the layers of story. But it is exciting—and this exhilarating experience is what not only draws us to storytelling, but makes great movies.

CHAPTER EIGHT

Critical Thinking and Creative Tools

IMAGINE reading thousands of scripts. And imagine meeting most of the writers behind these scripts, interacting with them socially, either as an executive, as a producer, as a writing colleague, in a formal class as an instructor, or as a script consultant. Each script is unique, reflecting the experiences of each writer, but the interesting pattern that emerges in the social experience is that each writer approaches the process of storytelling using their best critical thinking and creative tools, which are innate to their personal character, mind-set, and thought process.

THE EIGHT CREATIVE AVENUES INTO STORYTELLING

Based on these experiences, I have found that there are eight avenues that writers use to break through the screenwriting process. Although storytellers must eventually develop all eight avenues of critical thinking and creative tools, most writers have a few strong personal traits that dominate their thought process and are gradually able to develop the other avenues as they embrace the storytelling process.

When I explain these eight dominant avenues to my classes, I have found it helpful to personify the distinct approaches. Not only do these characterizations demonstrate the process of "morphing ideas" into characters, they also "characterize" the various problem-solving approaches in the storytelling process. Also, the choice of gender and order in which they are presented are specific to the thinking process involved, emphasizing the importance of each approach alone, and in contrast with the others. The more familiar you become to the storytelling process, the more you will appreciate how they work together as a creative team inside your mind:

- *Dr. Logic* is the holder of the moral compass of the story. He follows the continuity of story progression, establishing the moral dilemma through to the moral of the story. Dr. Logic holds very strong ideals about life, which is why he understands that when the main character goes "off story," it means the writer has lost focus on the moral dilemma. When the "Logics" listen to stories, they hear the details in the context of whether the story makes logical, moral sense.

- *Mrs. Spine* is the heart of the story. She is ultrafeminine, intuitive, and sensitive in approach, compassionate to the shortcomings of her fellow man. Born with the temperament to accept that all human beings are struggling and imperfect, Mrs. Spine doesn't care much for logical argument; she prefers poetic insight and understanding. The "Spines" tend to go "off-story" on a regular basis, but it's always in pursuit of discovering something fascinating about the human condition.

- *Captain Willful* is the creator of the main character. He intuitively knows how to present conflicts and challenges to drive the story through the main character. He is clear and precise about creating a state of mind, action, behavior and deeds. By knowing his own personal boundaries, he knows *exactly* what the main character will do and say, and exactly what the main character *will not do and say.* The "Willfuls" emphasize character-driven story structure and they know how to write for movie stars.

• *Professor Freud* is a problem solver who uses supporting characterizations to explore the main character's story. He is wily and insightful, yet sympathetic and kind to human failings, challenging the conflict within the story by creating supporting characters, scaling them back, eliminating some, and building them up again to tell the story. Endlessly fascinated by human nature and its paradoxes and contradictions, the "Freuds" express a deep appreciation of humanity by creating character-driven behavior and "voicing" their unique characters with an original tone.

• *Baby Brainstorm* is an idea person, gifted with the ability to problem-solve using visual and conceptual solutions, as opposed to internal and external character conflict. The "Brainstorms" are gifted with the potential to become great storytellers because they problem-solve with conceptual thinking that translates into visual solutions that can prevent disaster in the post-production phase.

• *Mr. Plot* works concretely with mechanics, devices, and techniques. He can unravel plots that make no sense and reconstruct them with amazing clarity. He epitomizes objective reasoning and mathematical certainty. Blessed with an amazing capacity to turn chaos into organized structure, he creates plots, subplots, and counter-plots freely and effortlessly. The "Plots" are always surprised to discover there is an abstract meaning behind the plot. For them, it's like opening a spectacular treasure chest of ideas.

• *Miss Wiggle* interrupts the flow of logical thinking in delightful and sexy ways. Fascinated by subtext, the "Wiggles" work with inference and surprise. By nature, they are comedic, able to conceive and construct original characters, and fantastic scenes that create word-of-mouth buzz around the picture that sells tickets at the box office. Story progression is a painful process for the "Wiggles" because story logic just doesn't enter their minds. Everybody loves

Miss Wiggle, and everybody needs her. The trick is to let her get her beauty rest while the others take center stage and establish the fundamentals of the story. Let her make her debut when she's good and ready. The "Wiggles" often work in teams, and they make great collaborators.

• *Sister Mary Story Synthesis* is extremely disciplined, with the capacity for synthesis of story. She knows when and how to call the creative shots, efficiently using critical and creative tools, shifting from one to the other, putting them aside according to the problem at hand, and integrating the avenues of critical and creative thinking tools effortlessly. People might mistakenly label this type of person as loose, but in fact, the "Synthesizers" are emotionally and intuitively absorbing what the story is about as they are creatively analyzing the missing story elements and logically constructing the progression of the dramatic story.

LEFT BRAIN–RIGHT BRAIN

In storytelling, an infinite number of questions can arise within a story, provoking an infinite number of possible answers and creative solutions. We often hear writers simplify this process of problem-solving by comparing left brain–right brain approaches. The left brain is the hemisphere of the brain responsible for logic, problem-solving, and linear thinking, geared toward finding the most efficient solution to a problem; whereas the right brain is the hemisphere that functions intuitively and emotionally to provoke original possibilities and creative solutions. For storytellers, the neuro-pathways of the brain are constantly exercised on multiple levels because storytelling integrates emotional content through multilevel mathematical and verbal problem-solving.

....

LEFT BRAIN

Dr. Logic uses reason and logic to guide the truth of the story.
Mr. Plot applies rational thinking to ensure that the story
events are inevitable.

FAVORING LEFT BRAIN–RIGHT BRAIN

Captain Willful personifies what the story is about
through the main character.
Sister Mary Story Synthesis unites all the story elements
through the spine.

FAVORING RIGHT BRAIN-LEFT BRAIN

Professor Freud uses characters and behavior to problem-solve.
Baby Brainstorm creates visual concepts and solutions.

RIGHT BRAIN

Mrs. Spine uses intuition and insight to guide the truth of the story.
Miss Wiggle interrupts the logic and predictability of the story.

....

Developing your creative team

All eight avenues are necessary to the storytelling process and work in harmony with one another. When they collide, intersect, and support one another, it creates magic. When one is missing, the story cannot move forward, let alone come alive with depth and humanity. Trouble erupts when Dr. Logic relies too heavily on Mr. Plot and "scene-writing" gets in the way of story progression. Everybody needs Mrs. Spine and loves Miss Wiggle, but very little gets accomplished when they spend the day together. Baby Brainstorm is loaded with ideas and visual solutions, but he needs Captain Willful to stay focused on the main character, who drives the story. And Professor Freud is fascinated by conflicts and choices, but he needs Sister Mary Story Synthesis to develop the progression of dramatic events through *character-driven story structure.*

Working with these eight tools is a wonderful, dynamic process. It begins with recognizing the value of each, and evolves into the art form of appreciating how they work together as a creative team. Understanding this flexibility within the human mind is one of the most exciting intellectual discoveries that we make as storytellers. Engaging in different ways of thinking is a wonderful way to bring out the best in your story.

PART TWO

Screenplanning

"How does my story make the audience feel?"

CHAPTER NINE

Genre

DECIDING *how to tell the story* is one of the most interesting elements of screenwriting. In fact, this important decision distinguishes screenwriting from writing plays and novels. As screenwriters, we must to choose the genre, or *category of composition of how to tell the story, characterized by specific style, form, and content.*

To understand genre, first and foremost you must understand that people go to movies looking for permission *to feel a certain way.* Many people decide what movie they want to see based on genre. Without a doubt, the ideal way to write a screenplay is to create a big idea first, and then decide which genre to use to tell the story. However, especially when you are starting out, you may choose the genre first, and then create a big idea and adapt that idea into the story you want to tell.

....

Genre is the category of composition of *how to tell the story.*
Genre is characterized by specific style, form, and content.

....

In practical terms, genre storytelling signals to the audience how they are supposed to feel from beginning to end. It guarantees that certain rules and expectations of that genre will be met. This is great news for screenwriters—because genre rules allow us to lean on the obligatory scenes and story points required by the established genre—giving us basic guidelines and conventions to work with as we shape an original concept into a story concept for a movie.

GENRES AND SUB-GENRES

Action

In action, the lead character's mission is enormous—sometimes literally to save the world. By self-sacrifice and by his wits, he succeeds against major obstacles and major villains. And he usually gets the girl—if he takes time out to meet one! *Rambo, Delta Force, Death Wish, Con Air, Code of Silence, Commando, Double Impact, XXX, The Dirty Dozen, 48 Hours, S.W.A.T., Die Hard, Lethal Weapon, Bad Boyz,* and *Dirty Harry* are unforgettable action movies.

Action-Adventure

In action-adventure, the lead character sets off on a simple mission in an adventurous world, comes up against a formidable villain, and often faces an adversary of the opposite sex. The lead character stays focused on the mission, and in the end, gets the girl. *Cliffhanger, Mission: Impossible,* the James Bond films, *Patriot Games, Clear and Present Danger, Air Force One, The Fugitive, Raiders of the Lost Ark, Billy Budd, Apollo 13,* and *The Great Escape* are male appeal action-adventure.

Romancing the Stone appeals to both genders as action-adventure, while *Thelma & Louise, Charlie's Angels,* and *Lara Croft: Tomb Raider* are female-driven action-adventure movies.

Animation

In animation, there is a simple story with a classic theme, lots of action, and the distinct possibility that characters and places can visually transform into something else. *Beauty and the Beast, Bambi, The Lion King, The Little Mermaid, All Dogs Go to Heaven, Cinderella, American Tail,* and *Spirited Away* are just a few of the best-loved animated features.

Art Film

The art film is conceived and developed outside the studio system, usually by one individual with a strong personal "voice." The uniqueness of the story is usually conveyed in strong visual and poetic terms: *Like Water for Chocolate, Babette's Feast, Talk to Her, 400 Blows, The Red Balloon, Jules and Jim, All About My Mother,* and *Cinema Paradiso* are good examples of this genre.

Comedy

In comedy, the lead character sets out to accomplish a goal, sometimes as simple as falling in love. The lead character overcomes larger-than-life obstacles to reach that goal, and gains greater appreciation for his values and loved ones along the way. There are many comedy sub-genres that allow for the uniqueness of voice and theme. Romantic comedies such as *When Harry Met Sally, Sleepless in Seattle, What a Girl Wants, How to Lose a Guy in 10 Days, You've Got Mail, Annie Hall, Bringing Up Baby, The Philadelphia Story, The Palm Beach Story,* and *It Happened One Night* appeal to all ages. High-concept comedies usually do very well at the box office; some examples are *Beverly Hills Cop, Dumb and Dumber, Down and Out in Beverly Hills, Analyze This, Some Like*

It Hot, Animal House, Bringing Down the House, Outrageous Fortune, Revenge of the Nerds, American Pie, Ed TV, Sister Act, Groundhog Day, and *The Out-Of-Towners.*

Dramedies became popular in the 1980s with such films as *Broadcast News, As Good As It Gets, On Golden Pond, Terms of Endearment, Beaches,* and *Kramer vs. Kramer.* Character-driven comedies usually succeed when they feature popular movie stars: *M.A.S.H., Tootsie, Big, Annie Hall, Manhattan, Caddyshack, Stripes, Private Benjamin,* and *Ace Ventura.* Farce does well in America, but not necessarily in the worldwide market: *Blazing Saddles, Bowfinger, Any Which Way But Loose,* The Marx Brothers, *A Fish Called Wanda, Austin Powers,* and *Fawlty Towers.*

Black comedies have specific appeal, usually to filmmakers rather than main stream audiences: *American Beauty, Dr. Strangelove, Network, Throw Momma from the Train, Harold & Maude, Get Shorty,* and *Men In Black.* Teenage comedies are among the most successful comedies because they ensure repeat audiences, especially if they are high-concept: *Clueless, American Graffiti, American Pie, Revenge of the Nerds, Ferris Bueller's Day Off, Back to the Future, Diner,* and *Stand by Me.*

Drama

In drama, the lead character confronts complex human emotions such as love, betrayal, jealousy, and envy, which are usually expressed through the potential or actual loss of a loved one, and sometimes the loss of material possessions. In the end, the lead character overcomes the internal emotional conflicts and earns a greater appreciation for life's struggles as well as the moral values that are tested along the way. Love stories are among the all-time favorite movies, especially when the lovers do not end up together: *Love Story, Out of Africa, While You Were Sleeping, Like Water for Chocolate, The English Patient, Wuthering Heights,* and *Random Hearts.* Thematic dramas usually attract attention-interesting actors: *Seabiscuit, Chocolat, A Streetcar Named Desire, A Few Good Men, Searching for Bobby Fischer, Quills,* and *The World According To*

Garp; and so do psychological dramas: *The Hours, Philadelphia, Spell-bound, The Swimming Pool, Sea of Love,* and *Vanilla Sky.* Some of the most popular movies ever made are dramas with tragic overtones: *The Godfather, The Manchurian Candidate, Casino, Raging Bull,* and *All The King's Men.*

Family Appeal

The family appeal movie explores child-centered themes, with adult-appeal references and often features animation and special effects: *The Wizard of Oz, E.T., Home Alone, Harry Potter, The Lord of the Rings, Spirited Away, Shrek, The Parent Trap, Heidi, Fly Away Home, A Christmas Carol, Flubber, Spy Kids,* and *It's a Wonderful Life.*

Fantasy

In fantasy, the lead character is transported to a fantastic world that is visually exciting and completely original. A traditional simplistic theme is enacted with larger-than-life villains and antagonists along the way, and the triumphant ending usually brings the lead character a profound inner realization. *Shrek, Shrek 2, The Lord of the Rings* and its sequels, *Ghostbusters,* and older movies such as *Cocoon* and *Harvey* epitomize the fantasy genre. Family movies such as *The Wizard of Oz, E.T.: The Extra-Terrestrial,* and *Harry Potter* appeal to child-friendly fantasies about home, family, and friends.

Female-Driven

Although this is a relatively new genre, it seems to be growing in appeal at a faster rate than other genres. *Thelma and Louise* led the way, followed by *Steel Magnolias, Waiting to Exhale, The Joy Luck Club, The First Wives Club, Stepmom, Fried Green Tomatoes,* and *Divine Secrets of the Ya-Ya Sisterhood.* The earliest female-driven movies are character-driven: *All About Eve* and Claire Booth Luce's *The Women.* Contemporary audiences, however, enjoy female-driven action pieces such as *Lara Croft* and *Charlie's Angels*.

Film Noir

The *film noir*, translated as "black film," features a man who is overwhelmed by a femme fatale who uses her charms to manipulate him for her own purposes, usually to do away with him for financial gain: *Double Indemnity, Farewell, My Lovely, The Maltese Falcon, The Postman Always Rings Twice, Sunset Boulevard, Touch of Evil,* and *Body Heat.*

Historical Epic

The historical epic features a hero against the backdrop of a major historical event. *Lawrence of Arabia, Reds, Schindler's List, Braveheart, Michael Collins, Gandhi, Patton,* and *The Last Emperor* are biographical epics, whereas dramatic epics include *Gone With the Wind, Ben-Hur, Gladiator,* and *The Ten Commandments.*

Horror

In a horror picture, a supernatural element threatens the lead character, who is drawn into a confrontation with good and evil. To survive, he must defeat the evil in himself as well as that of his primary antagonist. *Friday The 13ᵗʰ, The Omen, Carrie, Rosemary's Baby, Hannibal,* and *Night of the Living Dead* are classics of this genre. *Jaws* is one of the most memorable horror pictures ever made because it was the first of this genre to succeed as a crossover movie with family appeal.

Martial Arts

Martial arts movies appeal to worldwide audiences, especially films featuring Jackie Chan: *Crime Story, Project A, Dragon Strike, Police Force,* and *Drunken Master.* Bruce Lee is also popular: *The Curse of the Dragon,*

Fists of Fury, and *Dynamo.* Jean-Claude Van Damme has a strong international following: *Double Impact* and *Death Warrant.*

Musical

The musical explores a big theme with larger-than-life characterizations and splashy production numbers: *Chicago, Amadeus, The Sound of Music, Mary Poppins, Singing in the Rain, West Side Story, All That Jazz,* and *Grease.*

Science Fiction

Science fiction is a thinking person's genre that offers tremendous possibilities to make a social, philosophical, or political statement. This may account for the number of appealing sub-genres within science fiction. Alien invasion is one of the most popular themes: *Independence Day, Close Encounters of the Third Kind, The Thing, Mars Attacks!, The X-Files,* and *Alien.* Loss of identity attracts mainstream audiences: *Invasion of the Body Snatchers, The Matrix,* and *Superman.* Time travel has mass appeal: *The Time Machine, Back to the Future,* and *Timeline.* Fear of technology often attracts top-level directors: *The Terminator, Jurassic Park,* and *2001: A Space Odyssey.* End-of-the-world themes and space adventures do very well at the box office: *Dr. Strangelove, Testament, Armageddon, Star Trek, Alien, Star Wars,* and *Galaxy Quest.* Utopia and dystopia themes attract intellectual audiences: *THX1138, 1984, Brazil,* and *A Clockwork Orange.*

Suspense

In suspense, the lead character is on edge from beginning to end, gradually discovering what we already know: that the person closest to him or her is not only capable of murder, but plotting to murder him or her without any consequence. *Gaslight, Psycho, Rebecca, Single White Female, Rear Window, Vertigo, The Lady Vanishes, The Shining, Rever-*

sal of Fortune, Seven, and *The Hand that Rocks the Cradle* are some of the best-loved suspense pictures.

Thriller

In a thriller, the lead character tries to stay alive, on the run from his nemesis, trying to put together the pieces to uncover a hidden sinister plot, and ultimately, overcoming his nemesis. Smart thrillers engage the audience on an intellectual level: *North by Northwest, To Catch a Thief, The Italian Job, The Usual Suspects, Day of the Jackal, Spy Games, Absolute Power,* and *The China Syndrome.* Romantic thrillers stand the test of time and make great date movies: *Ghost, Rebecca, Mulholland Drive, The Talented Mr. Ripley, What Lies Beneath,* and *Double Jeopardy.* Psychological thrillers dominate the box office: *Basic Instinct, Fatal Attraction, Memento, Taxi Driver, Reversal of Fortune, The Bad Seed,* and *Play Misty for Me.* Techno-thrillers attract major directors: *Jurassic Park, A.I., Eyes Wide Shut,* and *Minority Report.*

War and Anti-war

Although war is often the setting for a love story, there are war pictures that actually feature war itself by honoring the heroes who risk their lives for the greater good: *Tora, Tora, Tora, The Longest Day, Glory, Hamburger Hill, The Great Escape, The Bridge Over the River Kwai, Sands of Iwo Jima,* and *Gettysburg.*

Anti-war movies use war or conflict to present an anti-war sentiment, rather than being about the heroes who risk their lives for a just war: *Das Boot, M.A.S.H., Apocalypse Now, Platoon, Coming Home, Born on the Fourth of July,* and *Dr. Strangelove.*

Western

The Western has exceptionally strong moral underpinnings, with a powerful main character at the center of a story with a strong personal mission. *Stagecoach, High Noon, Shane, McClintock, Jericho, How the*

West Was Won, Red River, and *Magnificent Seven* are classic Westerns. *Unforgiven, Dances with Wolves, Tombstone, Young Guns, Maverick,* and *Open Range* are contemporary Westerns.

IMITATING GENRE VS. IMITATING MOVIES

A word of caution to those who try to imitate great movies by studying a genre, choosing a movie prototype, breaking down the structure, and literally imitating the plot points, character functions, and conflicts of great movies: While studying great movies may be a good learning tool, imitating any movie—or imitating great lines from other movies—is plagiarism. More important, this misguided approach will interfere with your growth and development. Your work will feel derivative. Agents, managers, and gatekeepers are looking for originality even if it is expressed in a tried and true genre.

There is such a thing as writing a screenplay that is too "quirky" or "outside the system," especially with your first few scripts. Although this type of screenplay may get rejected, and it hurts, the agent or producer will be absolutely certain you wrote an original script. Ironically, being rejected for being "too quirky" means you have a unique voice, which is a great gift.

MASTERING GENRE VS. EXPLORING GENRE

Because screenwriters strive for originality, the notion of mastering genre is not a worthy goal. It is better to focus on exploring the elements of genres and sub-genres, learning to respect the rules, conventions, and expectations of each genre, and *letting the originality of your concept, character, and world where the story takes place speak for itself.*

MIXING GENRES

One of the most commonly asked questions is, "Can I mix genres?" Mixing genres may sound like a great idea, especially when you are attempting your first screenplay and trying to come up with something original; in certain cases, this bold effort may actually work quite well. In execution, however, you can also end up with a big idea that falls flat because the reader or audience *does not know how to feel about the story.*

By way of clarification, sometimes there are movies with crossover appeal that seem to fit into more than one genre, but if you look closely at how the movie makes the audience feel, one genre is dominant. For example, *The Wizard of Oz* is fantasy in the family appeal genre because it makes us feel there is no place like home. The same could be said for *Fatal Attraction,* which is a suspense piece that depicts a dramatic morality tale and makes us feel that marital fidelity is the cornerstone of a happy marriage.

Q: "Can I mix genres?"
A: Only if your name is Steven Spielberg or James Cameron.

This is an area where you can learn from the great filmmakers. Let's take a few examples of high-profile movies that may have communicated well to esoteric audiences but did not communicate the depth of their compelling concepts to the masses because they were told in mixed genres:

A.I.

This is a magnificent big idea about artificial intelligence, with a fascinating opening. It developed rather nicely with strong characterizations and then splintered into several storylines—transposed into a visual symphony rather than a traditional story. Although it was visually compelling, there were three stories being told at once, mixing fantasy, thriller, and science fiction genres.

Eyes Wide Shut

This is another extraordinary big idea, with a compelling situation about a man caught between his traditional life as a doctor and loving husband versus his deep fascination with a secret world of debauchery and corruption. What an appealing internal conflict and what a bold way to explore the world of the unconscious! But what was it all about? What was the narrative?

Solaris

Here is another potentially big idea that was universally appealing for its theme of romantic loss, but nobody knew quite how to describe the narrative of this story, let alone how to feel about it. This film could have been a psychological love story set against the cool, abstract world of outer space, but it ended up as a melodrama, under-dramatized and unromantic, not even science fiction.

If you, as an unknown writer, have written a script in a mixed genre, you will immediately know by the vague reactions from readers. "This doesn't work for me" is a popular complaint. Another might be, "I wasn't sure what it was about—it was hard to follow." Although this sometimes means the reader cannot literally follow the story, more likely it means they cannot understand *how to feel about your story*, and consequently, cannot relate to it or recommend it.

Above all, you must know what it is you are writing about, and how you want the audience to feel about your story. Movies make us feel intimate emotions in a communal way, and by choosing the best genre to tell your story you are helping your audience feel communal feelings about your story, moving you one step closer to communicating your story *as a storyteller.*

CHAPTER TEN

Plot vs. Story

ONE of the fundamentals of storytelling is to understand the difference between plot and story, and yet, this subtle distinction continues to stir confusion among writers. Plot and story may look the same on-screen, and in some movies, may feel the same to the audience, but in fact, plot and story are quite different from one another.

Plot is the Who, What, When, Where, How, and Why of the narrative. Plot choices are clear and precise and objective; they work together like a mathematical equation.

....

Plot is the Who, What, When, Where, How,
and Why of the narrative.
Plot = The concrete events of the story.

....

Story, by contrast, presents an infinite number of possibilities and layers to understanding the struggle of the main character as he or she faces a moral dilemma that intensifies with complications and obstacles as the story progresses.

....

Story is the synthesis of a moral dilemma of the main character
that intensifies with complications and obstacles through the
climax that reveals the moral of the story.
Story = The abstract meaning behind the plot.

....

PLOT

The plot is the main thread of the story, composed of the concrete events of the story, also called the narrative. The subplots are the little threads that support the plot, which function like tributaries feeding into one main river. Interestingly, the plot of a story can be filled with devices and choices that vary according to what the story is about and what you may want to say in your story. In other words, the plot shapes itself and mutates according to the story, not the other way around.

Nobody exits a movie exclaiming, "What a great plot!" When audiences respond deeply and personally to a movie, they exit crying or laughing, talking about the characters, usually the main character and what happened throughout the story. This is not to say that plot doesn't matter; rather it's to remind storytellers that plot is concrete and representational of the concept and story.

There are some writers with whom I have worked over the years who are extremely gifted at creating plots and subplots. This "plot-meister" talent works quite well in episodic television and journalism, but in dramatic long-form and feature films, this skill can sometimes interfere with a writer's growth and development. Creating subplots is only one aspect of creating a story. The process of storytelling is a complex effort of getting inside the story, discovering what it's about, and revealing the heart of the inner story.

STORY

Story is the abstract understanding that occurs in the audience as they identify with the moral dilemma of the main character, who is confronted with the weaknesses and challenges posed by his own moral weaknesses that represent those of the human condition. In theoretical terms, it is a synthesis of conscious and unconscious inferences that are gradually revealed as the moral of the story.

MASTERING PLOT AND SUBPLOTS

If you think of plot as similar to journalistic writing where the facts of the plot are presented as narrative through conflict, you will be able to master the basic understanding of plot. If you think of subplots as the little threads that support the plot, also presented as narrative through conflict, you will be able to structure a strong plot that moves forward with the momentum of supporting characters. Here are a few helpful guidelines to keep in mind during the "get started" phase:

- Commit to your main character. In movies, there is no story unless the audience knows the main character, identifies with his motivation, and can follow his goal.

- Commit to essential plot points. Essential plot points are concrete story events that are necessary to the telling of the story. The audience infers the meaning of the story from the plot points.

- Begin sketching the rising plot points that are necessary to advance the important plot points at the end of Act I, the mid-point, the end of Act II, and the climax.

• Create conflict and character-driven solutions that develop the plot and raise questions regarding what the story is about and suggest the spine of the story.

• Make sure all subplots have three story beats that reveal what the story is about thematically and recur throughout the main plot.

• Make sure all subplots support the main plot, or else get rid of the subplot.

• Make sure all subplots support the spine of the story.

THE HUMAN CONDITION

The *human condition* is a term that originated with French author-philosopher-Foreign Minister of Culture Andre Malraux's literary masterpiece *La Condition Humaine (Man's Fate)*, but has been adopted by contemporary storytellers to describe the chaos of the human soul. Malraux's novel, published in 1933, is set in the early days of the Chinese Cultural Revolution, and depicts the fictional account of a Chinese terrorist named Ch'en Ta Erh who struggles with the task of assassinating a sleeping man, as well as others caught up on both sides of the revolution. To this day, *La Condition Humaine* remains a powerful, classic tale because it is a story about free will and the liberty of man. From a storytelling perspective, however, it feeds the everyday vernacular of screenwriters.

DEVELOPING PLOT AND STORY

All writers begin somewhere, usually by evaluating ideas, sketching out characters, and creating conflict. If you find yourself a little blocked or overwhelmed, here is a checklist that will keep you on track:

✓ Commit to your main character, including his or her motivation, goal, and unconscious.

✓ Commit to essential story events, or plot points that convey the action of the story.

✓ Commit to key story points that reveal what the story is about thematically.

✓ Develop the spine of the story, remaining fully aware that this will evolve as you work inside the story with characterizations.

✓ Develop potential plot points that link the important plot points at the end of Act I, the mid-point, the end of Act II, and the climax.

✓ Establish the moral dilemma inside the main character through a character flaw, create conflict and character-driven solutions that feature the spine of the story.

✓ Reconsider the assembled plot points, always striving to come up with something more unique and original. Don't be afraid to throw an idea out and start over!

✓ Make sure all subplots have three story beats that reveal what the story is about thematically and recur throughout the main plot.

✓ Make sure all subplots support the main plot and reveal the story. Adjust or get rid of any subplot that does not advance the story.

THE ABCs OF SUBPLOTS AND STORY

Film and television executives often refer to A, B, or C stories, referring to the subplots within a story. The use of this terminology is often confused with the notion of the A and B stories, to differentiate between plot and story or to differentiate between the main character's external story and internal story. The problem with the confusion is that it opens the door for writers, even professionals, to create several subplots that do not support the main plot, splintering the story.

Based on my years of reading literally thousands of scripts, this is without a doubt one of the most common mistakes. There is one story. There is one main plot, but there are several subplots that support the main plot and reveal the story. While this may seem like semantics, it is crucial to understand the distinctions between plot, subplots, and story in order to create a "story" with unity of depth that plays on many levels.

....

There is one story.

There is one main plot.

There are several subplots that support the main plot

and reveal the story.

....

THE MORAL DILEMMA

The moral dilemma sets up the internal conflict of the main character. What is the primary decision he or she has to make throughout the story? Does it have the depth of a moral conflict? Or is it merely representational of an ethical conflict? A *moral conflict* reflects a problem that is related to the nature of man and questions of right and wrong, whereas an *ethical conflict* pertains to social mores or man-made issues and questions. The moral dilemma tests the main character's primary flaw through a difficult choice that, in larger terms, reflects the human condition.

CHAPTER ELEVEN

Creating the Main Character

PEOPLE go to movies to be entertained, and people want to see movie stars. They want to go places they have never been before and see characters that are larger than life, compelling, and fascinating. Although this may seem simple, if you keep these basics in mind, you will be headed in the right direction as you develop the main character of your story, who is also called the protagonist.

THE MAIN CHARACTER: CHARACTER DEVELOPMENT

As you create the main character, keep in mind that all human beings are a mixture of three major conscious and unconscious influences that affect character development:

Inborn Disposition

We are inherently different from one another by our innate chemical and physical make-up. Concurrently, the outside world reacts differently to these unique characteristics. In story terms, inborn disposition is innate personality that makes each character unique.

Life Experiences

As we move through the timeline of life, we are shaped by our life experiences, including our families, education, our loves, losses, setbacks, and accomplishments. Did we grow up in New York City? Peoria? Baghdad? London? Beijing? Dubuque? In story terms, the main character's life experiences that occurred prior to the story are called the back-story.

Projective Identification

As part of our evolution and development, we adopt the traits we admire in others in an attempt to acquire what they represent. In primitive cultures, hunters wear the skins of tigers to hunt game. In more "evolved" cultures, we define ourselves by maturity, which means a unique mixture of our *individual identification and projective identification,* which relates to the people in our lives who have been our role models for character traits we try to develop. In story terms, projective identification reflects the state of mind of the character.

Developing the main character is one of the most important objectives of the storyteller. One of the key factors is to resist creating a character that is fully mature, in favor of developing a character that is *struggling to become mature* as faced with the moral and social challenges presented in the story.

Persona vs. Arrested Character

Persona is the integration of character with the lessons in life, or maturity, which help us to develop into an authentic person with natural abilities, aptitudes, and character traits. In story terms, the main character's persona is plagued with a flaw, and as this flaw is tested throughout the story, the main character integrates a greater understanding of overcoming the flaw through the lessons of life that are expressed by the story.

Arrested character development, or immaturity, refers to those characters that remain imitations of others, and never quite develop into authentic human beings capable of attachment to others. In story terms, colorful villains and antagonists are always characters suffering from major arrested development.

The Story Elements of the Main Character

Creating the main character begins with creating a *state-of-mind*. This means establishing a world and a window into that world—through the main character—so that we, as the audience, can experience what he or she observes and hears. In concrete terms, it is almost as if we become the eyes and ears of the main character, filtering the world and characters of that world on his or her behalf. In story terms, this is called establishing identification with the main character.

Defining the goal of the main character is the next major element of the story related to characterization. Presenting an external choice or dilemma that forces the main character to establish his or her goal sets the character on course. If the goal is noble or heroic, we can follow his journey. If the goal is vague and uncertain, we get lost in nonscenes before the story even begins.

Establishing motivation is almost as important as defining the goal of the main character. Audiences like to understand motivation as quickly as possible, within the first ten to fifteen minutes of the movie. In one clear, concise moment they want to know exactly why the main character is doing what he or she is doing on-screen. In story terms, this is called "platforming" the motivation, which gives the audience a reason to follow the main character and supplies momentum to his goal or mission, such that the audience roots for the main character to accept the story challenge, against all odds.

Establishing identification with the main character differs from establishing point of view within the story. Establishing identification with the main character is achieved by revealing the state of mind of the main character and platforming his motivation.

Motivation must be emotionally powerful and absolutely clear.

Establishing point of view within the story means creating another character who interacts with the main character, and through conflict reveals the main character's internal struggle throughout the entire story. From a practical perspective, the point-of-view character is the character with whom you, as the writer, personally identify. The audience experiences your own personal voice within the story with emotional satisfaction. Not only are they following the main character, they understand what the story is really about.

Depicting internal conflict is a refined process of working with external character conflict to reveal the inner moral struggle. In effect, what you are trying to accomplish is to test the main character's moral fiber with increasingly difficult obstacles and standards against immutable unconscious drives. Experienced writers know that this is the most difficult story element to understand, let alone depict. Nonetheless, this "inner struggle" is what the audience emotionally identifies with throughout the story to its final conclusion. One of the most powerful recent examples of this is *Seabiscuit*, the true story of the extraordinary racehorse whose amazing ability to overcome enormous challenges inspired everyone who knew him. By the end of the movie, we have identified not only with *Seabiscuit*'s jockey, who motivates *Seabiscuit*, but we have internalized *Seabiscuit*'s own struggle, such that we feel amazed by his perseverance, inspired by his will to survive, and transformed by his determination to win against all odds.

Windows vs. State-of-Mind

There are many distinctive ways to portray characters on-screen, but two are generally preferred: windows and state-of-mind. Both are effective, and most writers and directors employ both, even in the same film. It is important to note that this is a matter of personal preference.

Windows are visual moments, as if we, the audience, are peeking through little windows, objectively watching the main character reveal himself. Using windows is similar to employing the omniscient perspective when writing a novel. Movies that use windows to convey character traits include *Chicago, Titanic, Star Wars, Harry Potter, Schindler's List, Forrest Gump, Home Alone, Lawrence of Arabia,* and *Out of Africa.* Steven Spielberg, Clint Eastwood, James Cameron, and Sydney Pollack consistently and reliably use this objective visual style throughout most of their movies.

State-of-mind moments are subliminal and subjective as if we, the audience, are actually living in the state of mind of the main character, experiencing his or her world. Using state-of-mind is similar to employing a first-person perspective when writing a novel. *Raging Bull, Amadeus, Diner, Jerry Maguire, American Beauty,* and *The Hours* are extraordinary examples of this style. Martin Scorsese, Milos Forman, Barry Levinson, Cameron Crowe, and M. Night Shyamalan consistently and reliably take us into the mind-set of their main character using this subjective style throughout most of their movies.

Sometimes filmmakers use windows and state-of-mind in combination, and we enthusiastically accept the end result: *Tootsie, Psycho, Rear Window, Fatal Attraction, Basic Instinct, Witness, Jurassic Park, Get Shorty,* and *Men in Black.*

ANTAGONISTS AND SUPPORTING CHARACTERS

Screenwriters who write character-driven action are in high demand because they know how to write for movie stars. One of the most interesting writers with whom I have worked is an actor who has appeared in numerous motion pictures and television series. He is born to write for the main character—but not an ordinary main character—a larger-than-life movie star hero that most mortals cannot imagine, let alone create. In the course of working with him, each week I would suggest that he needed a stronger antagonist and supporting characters to match the depth and excitement of his main character. Each week he would defy my suggestion by creating an even more exciting, forceful main character, and each week I would try to outsmart his main character with an equally forceful antagonist. We had a test of wills that created a bond between us as we attempted to outwit each other. Although this writer may not have known it at the time, he was teaching me as he was being taught, and the benefit was that the others in the seminar were learning the most valuable secret about storytelling: Your story is only as good as the antagonist!

CHAPTER TWELVE

Creating the Antagonist

STORYTELLERS love bad guys, really bad guys—the badder the better. The antagonist is the character who challenges the main character, tests the inner strength of the main character, and usually opposes the goal or mission of the main character. This power to contradict the main character is why the antagonist or antagonists can be the most exciting character(s) to create.

OPPOSING VALUES AND GOALS

The classic antagonist is linked to arrested character development, with primitive self-destructive traits such as envy, pride, jealousy, and narcissism. While the same three principles of characterization apply to creating the antagonist, the secret here is that *the strength of the story* is determined by featuring the antagonist's opposing values and goals:

- State-of-mind: inner conflict that opposes the main character

- Identifiability: real-life traits that are alluring, even if they are despicable

- Likeability (evil is good for the antagonist!): humorous and original

- Motivation: deep personal reasons that reflect arrested development

- Goal or mission: opposing the protagonist's

- Henchmen and allies (if part of the story)

- Love interest (if part of the story)

> The character formation of the classic antagonist is
> linked to primitive self-destructive traits
> such as envy, pride, jealousy, and narcissism.

The function of the antagonist varies according to the main character, or protagonist, which means the elements of characterization of the antagonist depend on the internal struggle of the main character. Also, depending on what kind of story you are telling and whether you're telling a classic hero story, anti-hero story, redemption story, or love story, the use of the antagonist will vary. Examples speak louder than words when it comes to villains and antagonists.

GREAT ANTAGONISTS

HANNIBAL LECTER (Anthony Hopkins) diabolically haunts FBI-trainee agent Clarice Starling (Jodie Foster) in *The Silence of the Lambs.*

In this psychological suspense-thriller, Clarice, the protagonist, is putting the pieces of a puzzle together to track down a serial killer, at the same time she is haunted by her past. Hannibal Lecter, the larger-than-life antagonist, is assigned to help her understand the workings of the mind of the gruesome killer who skins his victims; instead, Hannibal uses his evil cunning to penetrate Clarice's mind, seeking to manipulate her and destroy her fragile emotional state connected to her infantile relationship with her father—a relationship she is trying to overcome so she can let go of her painful past and emotionally integrate as a mature woman. Who can ever forget Hannibal Lecter? Hannibal Lecter pushes Clarice into maturity, while he triumphs as evil personified.

U.S. DEPUTY MARSHAL GERARD (Tommy Lee Jones) pursues Dr. Richard Kimble (Harrison Ford) in *The Fugitive*.

In this thinking man's action-adventure piece, Richard Kimble, the protagonist, is an innocent man on the run, wrongfully convicted of murdering his wife. Gerard, the antagonist, is matter-of-fact about his job to enforce justice by arresting and bringing in Kimble. However, in the course of pursuing his prey, Gerard's skepticism about Kimble's guilt evolves from doubt into curiosity, fascination, appreciation, and ultimately admiration for the fugitive, who is actually an epic hero in disguise. Ironically, Gerard's dogged pursuit of Kimble goads Kimble into vindicating himself by solving the murder of his wife.

ALEX (Glenn Close) slides into borderline madness by seducing family man Dan Gallagher (Michael Douglas) into an extramarital affair that escalates into a *Fatal Attraction*.

In this marvelous psychological thriller, Dan Gallagher, the protagonist, is a morally flawed family man who commits casual adultery with a woman who is not your average "other woman." Alex, a borderline personality with a troubled past, tyrannizes Gallagher by not accepting his termination of their affair. Alex threatens Dan's family, but as he experiences genuine and deep remorse for his infidelity, Dan recognizes that he loves his wife and family, and is willing to repair his marriage to save them.

DARTH VADER is the quintessential screen antagonist who challenges Luke Skywalker (Mark Hamill), in *Star Wars*.

In this classic good vs. evil story, Luke Skywalker journeys into manhood by saving his planet. Darth Vader, like Lucifer of the Old Testament, originated on the Light Side and has chosen to go to the Dark Side. Luke challenges Darth Vader and saves his planet, but cannot commit to destroying Vader. He allows Vader to live another day, perhaps in hope that this fascinating character, who is later revealed to be Luke's fallen father, will experience a crisis of conscience and abandon the Dark Side.

VILLAINS AND VILLAINESSES

While antagonists serve to oppose the inner struggle of the main character, villains serve to oppose the plot. In other words, antagonists are fully drawn like the main character, but villains and villainesses are deliberate scoundrels with minimal character development and dramatic motivation.

JACK NAPIER (Jack Nicholson), alias "The Joker" in *Batman,* is the completely sinister henchman of Gotham City's crime boss, Carl Grisson, whose wicked ways distract enigmatic millionaire Bruce Wayne/Batman (Michael Keaton) from rescuing Gotham City from crime.

THE WICKED WITCH OF THE WEST (Margaret Hamilton) in *The Wizard of Oz* tries to destroy Dorothy (Judy Garland) by preventing her, the Scarecrow (Ray Bolger), the Tin Man (Jack Haley), and the Cowardly Lion (Bert Lahr) from reaching The Wizard of Oz and getting help to return home to Kansas.

The glider-riding GREEN GOBLIN (Willem Dafoe) in *Spiderman* is the evil disguise of Peter Parker's best friend's father. When Parker (Tobey Maguire) is bitten by the mutant spider, he develops great powers as Spiderman, avenges the death of his uncle, and takes on the sinister Green Goblin, who seeks to destroy Gotham with his evil ways.

CRUELLA DeVIL (Glenn Close), the nasty, spiteful, self-centered woman in *101 Dalmations* is the epitome of vanity and the enemy of all dalmations.

Selfishly, she wants to skin the puppies to make a glamorous Dalmatian-skin coat.

THE TATTOOED SERIAL KILLER (Ted Levine) in *The Silence of the Lambs* is the off-screen villain and serial murderer who mercilessly skins his victims, fueling the events of the provocative story between Clarice and Hannibal Lecter.

DR. NICHOLS (Jeroen Krabbe) is the nasty hidden villain in *The Fugitive* who manipulates the FDA trials of a medication that causes liver failure, orchestrating the off-screen villains connected to the one-armed man who murdered Dr. Richard Kimble's wife (Sela Ward).

RON (Dabney Coleman), the soap opera TV director in *Tootsie,* is Julie's womanizing boyfriend who becomes Michael's (Dustin Hoffman) archnemesis. Although depicted humorously through his caddish behavior, Ron's "villainous" streak influences Michael to make some serious changes in his life and to become a better man.

THE WEIGHT OF THE ANTAGONIST

The quality of your story is directly related to the *weight of the antagonist.* This means that no matter how strong and unique your main character is, the story will not speak to the audience in powerful, dramatic terms without the weight of an equally strong opposing antagonist. Also, it stands to reason that the stronger the opposing character, the greater the dramatic force—or weight of the antagonist—within the story, the more entertaining and profound your story becomes for the audience.

CHAPTER THIRTEEN

Supporting Characters Who Tell the Story

IN great storytelling, each and every character is unique and original, and participates in the telling of the story relative to the main character. They also represent a variation on the theme, a dynamic aspect of the spine, and they serve the plot to advance the story. This requires developing the originality of each supporting character, with a personal history and background, as well as his or her own motivation toward a specific goal that supports or contrasts with the main character's motivation and goal. Ideally, even day players (who appear in one or two scenes) should be able to convey "actable attitude"—actions within scenes—that feed into the spine of the main character's motivation and goal.

Defining the dramatic function and thematic purpose of each character that is necessary to tell the story of the main character is an ever-changing process. When the story falls into place, story progression begins to emerge through conflict. Once you have achieved clarity of function and purpose for each character, then you can begin the art form of creating unique and original supporting characters.

··

All supporting characters conflict with the main character.
Conflict—both internal and external—reveals the story.

··

This checklist can assist you in determining how each character functions within your story:

The Main Character or Protagonist

✓ Is the leading character of the story.

✓ Consciously sets the external goal and embraces the mission of the story.

✓ Carries the central conflict, or moral dilemma, of the story.

✓ Experiences the most conflict throughout the story.

✓ Appears on-screen as much as possible throughout the entire story.

The Antagonist

✓ Opposes the main character.

✓ Attempts to foil the main character's external goal and mission.

✓ Causes the most conflict for the main character throughout the story.

✓ Appears on screen as much as possible throughout the entire story.

✓ Sometimes is more than one person.

The Love Interest

✓ Can function in more than one way (e.g., point-of-view character or antagonist).

✓ Is always connected to the main goal or mission.

✓ If he or she is also the antagonist, the love interest can function in opposition to the main goal or mission.

✓ If not, the love interest usually functions in conflict with, but in support of, the main goal or mission.

✓ Often causes the personal/inner conflict for the main character.

✓ Appears on-screen, as needed.

The Best Friend or Confidant

✓ Can function in more than one way.

✓ Usually supports the main character's goal and mission.

✓ Sometimes opposes the main character's goal or mission.

✓ Appears on screen only with the main character.

✓ There is a danger of losing conflict, or dramatic intensity, with this character, whose purpose usually supports the main character's goal.

The Antagonist's Best Friend or Confidant

✓ Supports the antagonist's goal to defeat the main character.

✓ There is a danger of losing conflict, or dramatic intensity, with this character, whose purpose supports the antagonist's goal.

The Catalyst or Story Agent

✓ Forces the main character into a different direction in the story, with a piece of information or a clue.

✓ Appears intermittently in the story, perhaps at three different times, to raise the stakes of the story.

Contrasting Characters

✓ Contrast with the main character, usually thematically and by action.

✓ Reveal specific traits of the main character, often as confidant or love interest.

Thematic Characters

✓ Reveal the depth of the story—what the story is about—by action.

✓ In genre pieces, there may be one or two thematic characters.

✓ In drama, there may be several thematic characters.

✓ In an historical epic, there may be many thematic characters.

The Point-of-View Character

✓ This is the character that you, as writer, choose to be the voice within the story.

✓ Interacts with the main character, reveals the inner conflict of the main character.

✓ Can function in more than one way, such as antagonist, contrasting, or thematic.

✓ The strongest character is the point-of-view character who is also the antagonist.

Day Players

✓ Butlers, valets, secretaries, chauffeurs, parking attendants who appear in one scene are called day players.

✓ They may appear insignificant to the story, but they can potentially raise the quality of the story by delivering thematic conflict with the main character and revealing the spine in subtle ways.

STRATEGIES FOR CREATING ORIGINAL
SUPPORTING CHARACTERS

Once you establish the dramatic purpose of each character relative to the main character and define how each character participates in the storytelling, then you can begin working within each character to develop originality through character action and uniqueness of voice. As writers, it is crucial to recognize that the dramatic purpose decision is key to the creation of original supporting characters. There are many ways to improve your ability to understand human nature and portray behavior that is authentic and interesting:

• Meet people: Believing that each and every person is unique and worthy of human dignity and respect is a sound philosophy for life. Socializing with this in mind is an excellent way to compassionately observe human behavior and develop an ability to depict original characters on-screen.

• Research: Reading magazines, periodicals, DEAR ABBY columns, psychiatric journals, newspapers, and novels are a good place to start. Developing an enriched intellectual life with an appreciation for the foibles of the human condition will open your mind to creating vibrant characters whom we have never seen before.

• Work against stereotypes: Although we live in a politically correct society, we live in a free society; one of its by-products is freedom of speech, which means we can invent and create any kind of characters we can possibly imagine. The key to working against typecasting is to understand the purpose and function of developing characters that challenge stereotypical social and political constraints.

• Listen to and watch live media: Talk Radio, Court TV, Jerry Springer, Don Imus, Phil Hendrie, Jay Leno, David Letterman, and just about any talk show in America brings out the worst and best in human nature. Keep in mind that publicists usually manage celebrities so they don't always have the go-ahead to project their own persona in the media. Ironically, some of the most original characters are ordinary people on the street who speak in their own unique, uncensored, animated voice!

• Use your personal experiences with others: Think about the people you know as if you were telling your own life story. There are some who bring out your sense of playfulness; others bring out your intellectual curiosity; others make you feel competitive; and others make you feel angry and defensive. When you want to reveal these traits in your lead character or any other character, call upon your own experiences to establish the uniqueness of your main character and supporting characters.

CHAPTER FOURTEEN

Creating Dramatic Conflict

ALTHOUGH you now have a big idea, story concept, main character, and budding antagonist, the story isn't quite there yet because you need to develop conflict within the story concept. This stage in the storytelling process is called *creating dramatic conflict*. The basics can be in place, but in order to complete the details of the plot and get to the story, you need to explore new levels of ideas to develop the material into the direction where it needs to go *as a story*.

This is a process where the ability to "brainstorm" and "wiggle" come into play. It's important to open up your mind to consider the full gamut of ideas you want to explore and break your patterns of thinking to conceive supporting and negating ideas that pertain to what your story is about. This will help you begin to discover the dramatic purpose behind your characters and create supporting characters to tell your story.

....

Consider the full range of ideas you want to explore,
so you can create the characters that you may need to
tell your story.

....

THE BASIC TASK

One of the major pet peeves of directors pertains to the primary task of writing. It is the job of the writer to explore the major possibilities within the story and eliminate the mediocre choices before the first draft. What this means is that, as the writer, you have to be willing to explore the "dialectic" of your story, which includes not only the "thesis" of your story, but as the Hegelian system suggests, *the "antithesis" of your story,* which encompasses the *opposing forces of the story.* In the course of this process, it is essential to formulate as many conflicting possibilities as you can imagine, and eliminate those that are ineffective, irrelevant, or superfluous in terms of story, before you begin the screenplay.

....

Creating dramatic conflict – creating the antithesis of
story concept.

....

What is left becomes the opposing forces of the story, which formulate the antithesis of your story concept.

....

The antithesis encompasses all the opposing forces of the story.

....

This process, or dialectic, of "thesis and antithesis" continues throughout, converges at the climax of the story, and resolves with a "synthesis" that reveals a practical lesson, or *moral of the story.*

"Dialectic" is the process of change in which a concept
or its realization
passes over into and is preserved and fulfilled by its opposite.
In Story terms, this dialectic repeats itself throughout Act II.

THE STEPS OF THE PROCESS

✓ What is the thesis of the story concept?

✓ What is the antithesis of the story concept?

✓ How does the thesis pass over into the antithesis?

✓ How is the thesis preserved and fulfilled by the antithesis?

✓ How are both the thesis and antithesis synthesized into the moral of the story?

Creating dramatic conflict = creating opposing story forces.
This is called the "antithesis" of your story concept.

THESIS + ANTITHESIS = SYNTHESIS (MORAL OF THE STORY)

Understanding this level of storytelling can be difficult, so let's look at examples that convey the abstract story progression of thesis, antithesis, and synthesis:

Titanic

Thesis
Rose (Kate Winslet) and Jack (Leonardo DiCaprio) come from different cultures, but it's their class differences and Rose's engagement to a wealthy man of social standing that keeps them apart.

Antithesis
Despite all the social and cultural obstacles, Rose and Jack unite in their love for one another; however, the forces of nature bring disaster on the ship, forcing Rose and Jack to test the depth of their love for one another in a race against time.

Synthesis
In the face of disaster, Rose rejects the financial comforts of a life with her wealthy fiancé, and surrenders her social and cultural status to be with the man she loves. Jack, despite trumped-up charges of thievery alleged by Rose's spurned fiancé, willingly sacrifices his life for others, including Rose, ensuring her eternal love and devotion.

Tootsie

Thesis
Michael (Dustin Hoffman), in his quest for fame and fortune as an actor, has become a cad, a narcissist, and a liar. Unable to find work because of his difficult personality, he puts on a dress, auditions as an actress named "Dorothy Michaels," and wins the role of hospital administrator Emily Kimberly in a soap opera. In order to succeed as an actor, he must give up his life as Michael, and live the role of Dorothy.

Antithesis
Michael, as Dorothy, falls in love with Julie (Jessica Lange), his co-star. Because Michael understands men better than Julie, he uses his identity as good-natured Dorothy to get to know Julie as best girlfriends and ad-

vises Julie about her dead-end romance with Ron (Dabney Coleman), the womanizing television director. Meanwhile, Dorothy, who becomes a hit with the public, meets Lester, Julie's father (Charles Durning), who falls in love with her. Now Michael, as Dorothy, is really in a pickle: He's in love with Julie, who has a beau, and at the same time, has become the object of Julie's father's affections.

Synthesis

Michael faces Julie and Lester with the truth about himself as Dorothy and Michael. However, his transformation back to Michael requires that he integrate the wonderful character traits he developed as Dorothy. As he begins to let go of the selfish, narcissistic aspects of his manhood, he earns the respect of Julie's father, Lester, and more importantly, the love of Julie.

The Fugitive

Thesis

Dr. Richard Kimble (Harrison Ford) has been convicted of killing his wife and sentenced to death; however, not only is he innocent, but a man of heroic deed and character. U.S. Marshal Gerard (Tommy Lee Jones) is charged to track down Kimble and bring him to justice. Gerard presumes Kimble's guilt, without any reference to Kimble's heroic character and good deeds. Dr. Kimble, in order to clear his name, must stay alive on the run, and solve the mystery by leading Gerard to the one-armed man who murdered his wife (Sela Ward).

Antithesis

Dr. Kimble's deeds and actions don't add up. Kimble is not acting like a killer on the run, he is flaunting his wits for Gerard's benefit, weaving in and out of public places, leaving clues in his wake that force Gerard to rethink the details of the entire case. Faced with contradictory evidence, Gerard begins, clue by clue, to question his task to bring in Kimble while at the same time admiring Kimble's impressive wits and generous deeds toward his fellow man. When Gerard is finally convinced that Dr.

Kimble is a man of integrity and decency, it's too late, because the one-armed man is connected to a host of villains who will stop at nothing to do away with Kimble.

Synthesis
Dr. Kimble pieces together the evidence not only against the one-armed man, but the host of villains behind the plot to murder Kimble's wife, and much worse. Gerard, against his better judgment, begins to respect Kimble, and reluctantly follows Kimble's set of clues, not only to the one-armed man, but to the hidden villains behind the deadly pharmaceutical plot. By remaining true to his good nature, Kimble solves the case for Gerard, reverses the injustice wrongfully cast upon him, and inspires Gerard to a new understanding of justice.

CHAPTER FIFTEEN

Moral Dilemma and the Moral of the Story

THE moral dilemma of the main character is one of the least understood elements of story, especially in relation to the spine of the story and the moral of the story. Let's begin with some basic definitions, before working with examples.

The word *moral* commonly refers to principles of right and wrong with respect to human behavior. In concrete story terms, a moral is the conclusion or lesson to be drawn from a story.

A *dilemma* is a choice of situations. In concrete story terms, a dilemma is a choice of situations involving equally unsatisfactory alternatives.

A *moral dilemma* pertains to the practical lesson we can derive from the choice of situations that challenge the main character as well as his or her capacity to understand right and wrong throughout the story.

The moral dilemma of the main character is sometimes referred to as the *central dramatic conflict* of the story. It raises a deep, penetrating question about the internal world of the main character, not only about his or her personal situation and flaws, but how this conflict, which is morally based, reflects our greater humanity.

MORAL VS. ETHICAL

It is important to distinguish between the meaning of the word *moral* and the meaning of the word *ethical,* as applicable to story.

Moral refers to absolute notions of right and wrong in
human behavior.
Ethical is related to good and bad in principles of conduct.

Storytelling imparts lessons in human behavior through character conflict with absolute moral ideals that are universal. In other words, all human beings have failings, and good stories feature these human failings in simple terms that help us understand life.

CREATING A MORAL DILEMMA

The unfortunate truth is that very few movies stay with us emotionally after we leave the theater. The reason we so willingly forget them is that, despite some entertaining moments, there is nothing memorable about the story. To create a story with lasting power, first we must establish what the story is about. This requires creating a character flaw in the main character, one that is clearly revealed as the basis of the dramatic situation and tested throughout the story.

The main character's flaw becomes the basis for
the moral dilemma.

When the main character confronts the antagonist(s) and story complication, we identify with his moral choice and understand the many levels of conflict that challenge the main character, including the motives of supporting characters.

CREATING SPINE THROUGH THE MORAL DILEMMA

In the same way that the main character and antagonist conflict with one another to reveal the moral center of the story, philosophers have used this method of playing one idea off of another to discover a greater truth about the world we live in. We owe this approach of using the conflict of opposites to the nineteenth-century German philosopher Georg Hegel, whose "Hegelian System," sometimes referred to as "dialectical philosophy," emphasizes that a system of philosophy must achieve some sort of absolute truth. By studying history, Hegel was the first to describe history as a process—opposing thoughts coming into conflict to birth a new thought that is then countered and so on.

Creating spine is like studying history. You begin with an idea or understanding of what you may think has happened, but as you assemble all the characters, events, details, facts, ideas, and underlying conflicts related to the historical event, you begin to *absorb the inner story* of what really happened.

Spine emerges from the main character's moral dilemma. The main character's flaw is always in conflict with absolute moral ideals.

What emerges from this intuitive, subjective experience represents a "key" that reveals the internal struggle of the leading character against absolute moral ideals. For example, we might view World War II through Winston Churchill's struggle to stay sober as he preserves the freedom and liberty of western civilization: "Never, never, never give up!" Or we may approach the Civil War through Abraham Lincoln's inability to cure his wife's madness as he heroically saves the Union by defining freedom and dignity for all men: "A house divided cannot stand."

While this process may seem abstract at first, the challenge is to break it down into workable steps, so you are able to navigate potential avenues into the story. As you begin to discover what the story is about from the inside, you can create character behavior that tests the moral dilemma of the main character, and by intensifying his moral choices throughout the story, you are creating story points that comprise the full argumentation, or complete synthesis, or spine, of the story.

Spine is the complete synthesis of the story.
All ideas, characters, and behavior support and oppose one another throughout.

THE MORAL OF THE STORY

The moral of the story is the message we take away from the film after the credits have run. The ideas, characters, and their behavior contribute to our understanding of what the story can mean to us on a personal level.

The beauty of a good story is that moral clarity requires no explanation because it is in complete balance with both the nature of man and the moral ideals of man. In fact, the moral of the story is the *final synthesis* of the spine of the story, wherein all the dramatic argumentation has been resolved.

Spine reveals the moral of the story.

Each of the following movies begins with a main character whose flaw is revealed through a clear moral dilemma. The story is synthesized through spine, which reveals a meaningful and powerful *moral of the story.*

Schindler's List

Character flaw
Schindler (Liam Neeson) is a narcissistic and self-serving man.

Moral dilemma
He is content to line his pockets with the help of the Nazis until he sees a little girl's life cut short. He makes a dramatic decision to turn his life around by putting aside his pursuit of wealth and prestige to rescue Jews, one life at a time.

Spine of the story
By surrendering his own interests for the greater good of others, Schindler becomes a truly decent man.

Moral of the story
His story teaches us that letting go of material pursuits and risking our lives for the survival and welfare of others is the pathway to a meaningful life.

Amadeus

Character flaw
Antonio Salieri (F. Murray Abraham) is envious, spiteful, and prideful.

Moral dilemma
Salieri attempts suicide to escape his envy, but lives to confess his sins, proudly taking credit for destroying the gifted Wolfgang Amadeus

Mozart (Tom Hulce). Despite absolution from a priest, Salieri chooses envy, which leads to self-destruction.

Spine of the story
By celebrating envy, Salieri decays from within, destroying his most valued gift—his talent.

Moral of the story
His story teaches us that envy robs us of our own artistic genius, and diminishes our capacity to transform ourselves into fully realized human beings.

The Godfather

Character flaw
Michael Corleone (Al Pacino) is a weak man, dominated by an overpowering father who is known by those who fear love and fear him as The Godfather. (Marlon Brando).

Moral dilemma
Michael meets Kay (Diane Keaton), who sparks his desire to give up his family's notorious lifestyle for peace of mind, but a family murder draws him back into the family tradition.

Spine of the story
By refusing to stand for integrity, Michael is condemned to lose everyone he truly loves and everything he values, including his soul.

Moral of the story
His tragic story teaches us that to be seduced by false notions—even family prestige—threatens the comfort of a clear conscience, and leaves us lonely, tormented, and devoid of happiness at the end of our lives.

Chocolat

Character flaw
Viviane (Juliette Binoche) is an unwed gypsy mother who has no apparent socioeconomic or religious basis for her life in a small French village.

Moral dilemma
She endures the unkindness, intolerance, and condescension of others, but her good works of love and kindness inspire the villagers to examine their own capacity to love one another.

Spine of the story
By compassionately loving others selflessly, Viviane's recipes for chocolate cure the villagers' suffering souls.

Moral of the story
Her magical story teaches us that all we acquire in life as human beings is the generosity we leave behind.

Die Hard

Character flaw
John McClane (Bruce Willis) longs to be a hero, but he's so lacking in courage, he's even afraid to fly.

Moral dilemma
He visits his ex-wife (Bonnie Bedelia) and children for Christmas, hoping to win back their affection—with a teddy bear. When he discovers a bomb threat plot in the building where his ex-wife works, he summons up the courage to risk his life, not only to save her, but to save the entire building full of people.

Spine of the story
By rediscovering his love and affection for his ex-wife and family, McClane recovers his courage to become a hero to himself and others.

Moral of the story
His story teaches us that even if you gain the admiration of the entire world, the safety, security, and love of your family is what endures.

My Big Fat Greek Wedding

Character flaw
Toula Portokalos (Nia Vardalos) is too timid to mature into a woman and separate from her family, who wants a big fat Greek wedding.

Moral dilemma
She meets a handsome Anglo-Saxon (John Corbett), and makes the decision to fall in love, but first, she transforms into a woman who must separate from her family in order to embrace romantic love.

Spine of the story
By letting go of spinsterhood in a Greek family, Toula invites the love of her life to rescue her from loneliness.

Moral of the story
Her story teaches us that love is where you find it, and it starts with loving yourself.

Mr. Deeds

Character flaw
Deeds (Adam Sandler), based on Frank Capra's *Mr. Deeds Goes to Town,* is the original nice guy. He appears to have no character flaw, except his inability to recognize character flaws in others.

Moral dilemma
He inherits a great deal of money and his integrity is tested by a series of conniving, deceitful people, in particular, a tabloid journalist (Winona Ryder) who pretends to care about him.

Spine of the story
By confronting the cruelty of others with kindness, Deeds overcomes his own weakness and inspires them toward kindness.

Moral of the story
His story teaches us that although standing up to malevolent people may be essential for survival, the strongest show of strength is the capacity to inspire others by treating them with dignity, respect, and generosity.

WEAK MORAL DILEMMAS

In contrast, here are examples of weak moral dilemmas from stories that are melodramatic or incomplete. This does not mean that these movie are not entertaining; it just means that there are no residual feelings connected to these films, and that they have no long-term potential as classics:

Terms of Endearment

The redemptive story of a mother and daughter at odds with each other, starring Shirley MacLaine and Debra Winger. This dramedy veers into soap opera with the daughter's cancer plot, which forces the mother-daughter reconciliation through a plot point rather than character growth.

Beaches

The story of two best friends (Bette Midler and Barbara Hershey) constantly competing with each other loses its comedic appeal when a cancer plot redirects the genre away from comedy to melodrama. Again, a plot point turns the story, instead of character growth, and the movie falls short of a classic.

The American President

The President of the United States (Michael Douglas) is dating a lobby-ist (Annette Bening). Nice notion, but the impropriety of the President-lobbyist relationship is an ethical consideration, not a moral dilemma, so what might have been a charming premise for a romantic comedy is reduced to melodrama before it takes off.

The Mirror Has Two Faces

Two professors (Barbra Streisand and Jeff Bridges), can't seem to fall in love because the man believes in celibacy as a basis for developing a meeting of the minds and the woman prefers the carnal route to inti-macy. This sounds like a smart gender-war movie, but plays like "polit-ically correct" wishful thinking. The audience doesn't buy the celibacy premise, especially when the leading lady is of a mature age and her love interest denies her romantic attention. Women experience it as re-jection, and men experience it as ludicrous.

Notting Hill

Julia Roberts plays a movie star struggling to fall in love with a com-moner (Hugh Grant). This is a sweet premise with two engaging movie stars, but there is nothing dramatically compelling about two attractive people who are reluctant to take an emotional risk. There is no dra-matic dilemma—let alone a moral dilemma—just a few cute scenes. Al-though mildly entertaining, this movie is forgettable.

Up Close and Personal

Michelle Pfeiffer plays an ambitious television journalist whose career is shaped by a veteran journalist (Robert Redford). They fall in love, marry, and a skirmish in Central America draws them apart. To its credit, this movie contrasts two lovers with strong motives and drives, but there is nothing substantial at stake, morally or otherwise—only a romantic separation due to a TV job covering a would-be war.

Two Weeks Notice

Hugh Grant plays a difficult boss, and Sandra Bullock doesn't want to work with him. This is a good little premise with lots of potential conflict, if only the leading man had a moral center. Without a strong leading man, it's difficult to break the box office.

The beauty of creating a powerful moral dilemma for the main character is that it opens up the levels of understanding *what the story is really about*. With a clear comprehension of the choices the main character faces throughout the story, you will be able to feature the key dramatic moments that contribute to the final synthesis, or moral, of the story.

CHAPTER SIXTEEN

Following the Emotional Story

SOME screenwriters, and many playwrights, begin with the emotional story, or *inner story*, rather than with a compelling situation or a strong plot. They layer key dramatic moments between the protagonist and antagonist in conflict with each other, creating heightened emotional moments—sometimes called *points*—that serve as climaxes and story beats. By intuiting the depth of character conflict, without emphasizing plot and structure, they work through the unconscious movement of the story by way of external character conflict, revealing "story" as a by-product. Tennessee Williams worked this way. So did Jason Miller. If this is the way you naturally work, this chapter will help get you off to a good start; however, remember that *in creating a screenplay,* you still have to do the "nuts and bolts" of developing a strong plot to support the external on-screen story.

By exploring and defining the unconscious internal conflict of the protagonist against the external forces of antagonism, key dramatic moments have a chance to percolate. This approach works particularly well in theater, which relies heavily on thematic characterizations, but in film, the ability to create visuals that tell the story is so crucial to the final product that a screenwriter must constantly transpose key emotional moments into images without dialogue.

Following the emotional story requires intuitive and analytical skills that serve the development of character-driven twelve-sequence story structure. In simple terms, this means creating *twelve major story points,* and staying with the main character's emotional story on-screen while developing the opposing forces of antagonism. To assist you in understanding this "inside-out" approach, let's look at a conceptual outline of the twelve-sequence story and identify twelve key emotional moments that can be mined for development. Keep in mind that the job of the writer is to think through the many and varied possibilities, and eliminate the mediocre choices. The key is to develop the full gamut of *"ideas as characters"* that contribute to the story, and then work within the characterizations to create emotional highlights.

SEQUENCE 1: ESTABLISHING MOTIVATION, MORAL DILEMMA, PERSONAL STORY

The writer's first chance to create a strong dramatic moment occurs with the opening image of the movie, but the first *emotional moment* of the story occurs when the writer establishes the motivation of the main character. If the motivation is depicted with primitive feelings such as loss, jealousy, or love, or envy, the audience will automatically identify with the main character throughout the entire story. As a result, the reader/audience will stay with the main character's story even if you make a few story missteps along the way. Conversely, if the main character is undermotivated from the very beginning, the story will feel like melodrama.

The second opportunity for an emotional moment in the first sequence is establishing the main character's moral dilemma. The audience already understands the basics of the main character's state-of-mind and motivation, but now, with two diverging paths presenting a difficult choice for the main character, the audience will see him or her take action, but by this time, they will be invested in the main character taking the path of most resistance. The secret here is to develop equal and opposing antagonism to both paths, such that the audience believes either path is viable, but hopes the main character chooses the more intriguing, dramatic, adventurous path riddled with the most conflict.

One of the most powerful human drives is to fall in love. Watching the main character surrender affection and desire to a love interest is the third opportunity in the first sequence to develop the emotional story. There must be something irresistible about the love interest that we understand in much the same way as the main character; something more than physical beauty; something emotionally alluring such as goodness, honor, loyalty, integrity, kindness, tenderness. Or, if you are writing a film noir or thriller, this attraction can be seductive, perhaps evil, or something psychologically compelling that we ourselves are reluctantly attracted to. More important, we must believe the main character is attracted to the love interest because she (or he) represents something of emotional value, something we want to become, or perhaps something we falsely admire and may unconsciously wish to become.

SEQUENCE 2: FIRST SCENE BETWEEN MAIN CHARACTER AND ANTAGONIST

A good storytelling strategy is to write the first scene between the main character and antagonist before you begin writing your screenplay. It proves or disproves whether your premise and dramatic situation are strong enough to carry the entire story. If you cannot write this scene, or if you don't know what this scene is about, then go back to the drawing board. Your story concept isn't far enough along to develop the emotional story.

SEQUENCE 3: MAIN CHARACTER'S KEY DRAMATIC DECISION

After introducing the story complication that opposes the situation, the writer depicts the main character's decision to accept or embrace the mission or goal. This scene—the main character's key dramatic decision—is another opportunity to test whether you can bring together motivation and the inner conflict of the main character through external character conflict. The secret here is to work with a thematic character to create external conflict that reveals the inner world of the main character, advances the action of the story, and explores various levels of spine.

SEQUENCE 4: MAIN CHARACTER'S FIRST SUCCESSFUL MOMENT

By this time, the main character is moving toward achieving his or her goal, so it may seem that writing the first successful moment would be easy, but often, this is one of the more difficult story points to create. In fact, this juncture is where many stories lose momentum for two major reasons: The main character is not fully motivated; and the forces of antagonism are not properly layered into the story. The challenge here is to make certain that these two requirements are in place so you can establish obstacles and use characters in friendly ways that move the action forward but come back to haunt the main character later in the story.

SEQUENCE 5: THE ANTAGONIST'S STORY THRUST

When you are constantly developing the antagonist's opposition to the main character, one of the most significant objectives is to develop the *antagonist's story thrust*. This story movement creates a chilling feeling or sense of skepticism in the audience by dramatizing the depth and strength of the antagonist's motives and goals, featuring exactly what the main character is up against, both morally and externally. Many screenplays fall flat here. The preferable choice would be to feature both the antagonist and the villain, as well as any subplot or character that opposes the goal of the main character or challenges the flaw of the main character.

SEQUENCE 6: SECOND MAJOR SCENE BETWEEN THE MAIN CHARACTER AND ANTAGONIST

This is one of the key emotional moments in the story, when the main character asserts his or her drive to achieve the mission or goal, in the face of the antagonist, whose strength and force are ascending and escalating. This where you have a chance to develop the most exciting set piece in the movie, this time favoring the antagonist.

SEQUENCE 7: MARSHALING THE FORCES OF ANTAGONISM

The last great scene at the mid-point featuring the antagonist was so exciting and emotionally wrenching, the key here is to raise the stakes for the main character and maintain the escalation of the forces of antagonism, so that there is no turning back.

SEQUENCE 8: GIVE MOMENTUM BACK TO THE ANTAGONIST

The antagonist is controlling the story now, and this is where the antagonist and his or her cadre of supporting characters take aim at destroying the main character. Few screenplays actually make it to this point because all the building blocks must be in place, but if you can make it this far, this is the time to depict the antagonist at his or her most sinister and the main character at his or her breaking point.

SEQUENCE 9: THIRD MAJOR SCENE BETWEEN THE MAIN CHARACTER AND ANTAGONIST

Screenwriters almost always write this moment, but they tend to jump straight into a big "set piece" scene that completes the "antithesis" of the story concept, without detailing and depicting the key emotional moments that lead up to it. It doesn't hurt to experiment with this scene in the early stages of writing the screenplay, but it is very important to recognize that this scene will continually be rewritten as you discover new and fascinating layers to the story.

SEQUENCE 10: RESURRECTING AND DEFEATING THE MAIN CHARACTER

If your screenplay is well constructed with key emotional moments developed in the first nine sequences of the twelve-sequence story, there will be many opportunities to develop an internal story movement here where the main character may even turn his or her back on the main mission or goal. At this time, you want to resurrect the main character's motivation and goal, and create a dramatic setback that is even more daunting than the defeat in the prior sequence.

SEQUENCE 11: THE MAIN CHARACTER AND ANTAGONIST PREPARE FOR THEIR FINAL CONFLICT

Again, if your screenplay is well constructed with a strong motivation and clarity of purpose for the main character, there will be many possibilities to work with. Developing key emotional moments for both the main character and antagonist as they shore up their wits and determination to defeat one other guarantees increased momentum of the story.

SEQUENCE 12: THE MAIN CHARACTER'S KEY EMOTIONAL MOMENT, CLIMAX, AND RESOLUTION

The most important emotional moment of the story occurs when the main character experiences insight with regard to his personal conflict or flaw, which moves him to a new understanding of his journey. This key emotional moment occurs just before the climax. It is—*and should be*—extremely difficult to write. In fact, the main character's final insight is usually written and rewritten many times until it rings true.

> The key emotional moment of the story occurs just before the climax.

The climax of the story follows, in the form of external character conflict. The main character, having triumphed over his moral shortcomings, triumphs externally over the antagonist, achieving the mission or goal of the story. More important, because the climax occurs at the point of story synthesis, the climax yields *a powerful emotional reaction* from the audience that requires no further dramatic explanation.

PART THREE

Screenwriting

"This is what my story is about."

CHAPTER SEVENTEEN

The One-Page Summary

MARKETING and publicity are crucial to the economics of the film business. One of the most important prerequisites involved in creating a movie is being able to know your story so well that you can convey your movie in a "one-page" summary of a few hundred words. This presupposes that you already know the basic characters, plot, and story. Nonetheless, writing a "one-page" can be so overwhelming that many professionals don't even make an attempt to write it until the screenplay is completed.

As a writing exercise, however, sketching out a "one-page" after you have worked through the major story conflict between the main character and antagonist is a smart move. It forces you to commit to your big idea in writing, such that you begin *telling a story,* as opposed to writing scenes. Ideally this "one-page" becomes the ultimate selling tool because it prepares you to orally pitch the story to interest a top literary agent who may, in fact, use this very same "one-page" to interest buyers.

While each project is unique and requires its own special approach, a "one-page" must cover at least four elements. Here is a "four-paragraph, one-page" structure that begins with a "hook" that invites an agent, director, or producer to read your screenplay.

THE "FOUR-PARAGRAPH, ONE-PAGE" STRUCTURE

Paragraph One

The first paragraph describes what the story is about, featuring the main character, the story premise, and story concept. This paragraph should also convey an image that communicates the story, depicting thematic forces within the story, especially the main character's internal conflict. This first paragraph, especially the film image, is very difficult to create, let alone write. In effect, it becomes the basis of the all-important "movie poster," which promises the audience what they can expect to feel about your story. If you haven't thought through the story on this level yet, don't worry. This is a tool to get you started. There will be changes, even after you have written the script.

Paragraph Two

The second paragraph goes straight into the narrative, giving a feel for the tone and style of the piece, the world where the story takes place, the fully realized lives of the main characters, and the dramatic events featuring the who, what, when, where, why, and how of the story. In structural terms, the second paragraph establishes the complete story concept, featuring the antagonist and story complication. In the twelve-sequence story structure, this paragraph features the story points of the first three sequences. In a traditional dramatic three-act structure, it would be the first act.

Paragraph Three

The third paragraph summarizes the essential story points of the second act of the story, which is the fully dramatized antithesis of the story concept. The secret to this paragraph is that the story beats must be concise, including character decisions, emotional moments, and dramatic events that depict the greatest number of story twists, turns, and plot reversals—in as few words as possible! Most stories fail somewhere in the second act, so if you do not have enough story for a movie, you will know by now. Conversely, if you have a great story that can become a movie worthy of major financing, the reader will already be looking for your phone number.

Paragraph Four—and Five, if necessary

The fourth paragraph builds toward the climax of the story between the main character and antagonist(s). Above all, this last paragraph—plus a fifth paragraph if necessary—must capture what the story ultimately is about, featuring the main character's final insight, or moment of realization, through the point-of-view character, driving the story to a climax and resolution that promise a greater human understanding or universal truth as revealed in the moral of the story.

Remember, this format is only a suggested approach that is meant to cover the basics. Each story has its own story and marketing requirements. For example, if there are underlying rights, such as a book or true story rights, you must note this as early as possible in your "one-page" and then quickly relay the details of the plot and story so that the reader has a good sense of the overall elements of the story and how your project fits into the current marketplace. By way of an example, if I were asked to write a one-page summary of James Cameron's *Titanic*, it would require more presentation than a typical feature film (five paragraphs, rather than four) because of its scope as a major epic:

TITANIC

The R.M.S. Titanic—*the "Ship of Dreams"—is a time and place where a poor boy and a society girl fall in love. Fate intervenes when the legendary "unsinkable" ship hits an iceberg and sinks on April 15, 1912, and the star-crossed lovers risk their lives for one another, cherishing each other unto death.*

The present-day mission to recover the R.M.S. *Titanic* recovers an erotic portrait of a young woman wearing a heart-shaped blue diamond. The woman in the portrait, 101-year-old Rose Dawson, steps forward and tells the tale of *Titanic* wherein eternal love triumphs over all: JACK DAWSON, after winning a trip on the R.M.S. *Titanic* in a dockside card game, fancies ROSE DeWITT BUKATER, a socialite who is on her way to Philadelphia to marry her wealthy fiancé, CAL HOCKLEY. As they board the ship, Rose and her ambitious mother marvel at the magnificent ship that has attracted 2,200 passengers on its maiden voyage, including the Guggenheims, the feisty Molly Brown, and the ship's builder, Mr. Andrews. Jack risks his life to save Rose, who dreads her marriage to Cal and attempts suicide by throwing herself over the railings of the ship. In recognition of Jack's courage and honor, Cal is obliged to invite Jack to join them for dinner in first-class. With coaching from Molly Brown, Jack rises to the occasion, and exits, leaving a note with Rose, inviting her to meet him at the clock at the top of the stairs. Rose and Jack dance passionately throughout the night in steerage. He sketches the erotic portrait of Rose wearing the diamond. They consummate their love, and together they embrace a dream of their own.

The next day, Cal sabotages Jack by slipping the diamond into Jack's coat pocket to set him up as a thief. Then suddenly, the crew gets news of an iceberg ahead. Mr. Andrews acknowledges there are two hours and forty minutes before the ship goes down, and not enough lifeboats for all the passengers. Just before they hit the iceberg, Cal discovers the portrait. He issues an ultimatum. Rose casts her lot with Jack, and Cal orders Jack under house arrest for stealing the diamond. Rose gives up her seat on a rescue boat, to save Jack. Wading through water, she releases him using an axe, but the crew has locked the third-class gate. Cal arranges a bribe to gain passage on a rescue boat while Jack and his friends crash through the gate, releasing hundreds of passengers. Cal persuades Rose to join him, with the false promise that there's a seat for Jack. When Rose realizes Cal has lied, she escapes with Jack, wearing his coat with the heart-shaped blue diamond.

Jack and Rose try to rescue a child, as Cal kidnaps a child and boards a rescue boat. Mr. Guggenheim prepares to go down like a gentleman, drinking a brandy, and the child Jack and Rose tried to rescue goes underwater. As the "Ship of Dreams" spikes downward into the sea, the priest blesses the souls of the lost passengers, and Jack and Rose plunge into the freezing water. The irrepressible Molly Brown insists fellow passengers transfer to another boat, so she can rescue others. Jack helps Rose onto a floating wood piece, promising not to let go. The next morning, amidst 1,500 frozen, lifeless bodies, Rose makes her way to a crewman with a whistle, and is rescued. Jack has died in the night.

Seven hundred survived. Out of twenty boats, only Molly's returned to rescue others. one-hundred-and-one-year-old Rose tosses the heart-shaped blue diamond back to the Titanic. *Her youthful vision of Jack—who "saved me in every way a person can be saved"—fulfills her dream of eternal love with the memory of a romantic kiss.*

The Step Outline

IN the past, until a few years ago, screenwriters under contract to the studios wrote "film treatments," which are abbreviated film stories of about five to fifteen pages. Today, most screenwriters begin with a story and then adapt the story into a structural form called the step outline.

....

The film treatment is a short version of the screenplay
written in story form.

....

The step outline has become a popular intermediary form between the "treatment" and "screenplay," especially among film companies and studios, because while many writers are able to come up with a great story concept, when it comes time to execute the concept, few can actually deliver.

The step outline develops your story in detail,
dramatic moment by dramatic moment.

Defining the inner workings of the "character-driven story structure" is the challenge of a professional screenwriter, and the purpose of a step outline is to convey the story dramatic moment by dramatic moment through the character's subconscious, personal, and external conflict.

The step outline is presented scene by scene, in story form.

If spine is "what your story is really about," how can you possibly write the step outline until you can answer this question? At this stage, it is safe to experiment with what your story is about, as if presenting an hypothesis as the basis for your story. As your level of understanding of what the story is really about increases, the spine will emerge from the main character's story.

STORY LOGIC AND EMOTIONAL IDEAS

You can begin your step outline by creating and organizing plot points and story points in a consecutive, progressive, logical order. This process requires the ability to develop a plot narrative that is based on cause and effect, relying on story logic. The sum total, or synthesis, requires filtering plot and narrative through the emotional ideas of the story that are represented by lifelike characters via the spine of the story.

Keep in mind that the dramatic moments—story beats—you create in a step outline may look like concrete scene moments, but they carry much more emotional weight. They are sketches of character trajectories, with goals and motivations, revealed through multiple layers of conflict that build a plot from which we can infer story. However, in storytelling terms, the scenes that feature the story beats are always changeable, interchangeable, and disposable. *It's the emotional weight of the story beats that matter in storytelling!* By weighting the story beats, you can emotionally absorb what your story is about as you are experimenting with and discovering the spine of the story. And when the spine starts to crystallize, you will appreciate that—through characters and behavior—there are many ways to create scenes and play the conflict. The storytelling plays on several levels such that you can create *dynamic scenes* as well as *dynamics within the scenes* that support, negate, and reveal the spine of the story.

FROM STORY BEATS INTO SCENES

Before committing your character-driven story structure into a written step outline, you must have four fundamentals:

1. Know what your story is about.

2. Tell the story through your main character, who faces a strong internal conflict and moral dilemma.

3. Establish the forces of antagonism that challenge your main character with external conflict.

4. Develop a story complication that serves the ongoing story by giving momentum to the second act through the climax.

From a practical viewpoint, some writers prefer to use 3 x 5 note cards to sketch story beats into scenes. Others prefer using a legal pad or computer. It doesn't matter which mode you prefer. The final product of written story beats should be five to six pages, with somewhere between thirty-five and forty-five story beats. The secret to creating the written step outline that works is: *Develop the story beats first, and then develop the story beats into scenes.*

STORY BEATS VS. SCENES

A *story beat,* sometimes called a *story point,* advances the abstract understanding of the story as well as the plot.

A *scene,* however, conveys a *story beat* or *story point* through a concrete dramatic scenario that includes a location, time setting, characters, visual images, theme, subtext, and dramatic conflict on several levels.

Scenes originate from story beats, which means you *must* create the story beats first. If you miss this distinction, you will paint yourself into a corner by creating scenes that interrupt the story progression. Going "off story" means you are having trouble understanding the difference between a *story beat* and a *scene.* It also indicates that you are having trouble expressing the abstract meaning of the story through the concrete representation of a series of scenes.

> Sometimes it takes more than one scene to complete a story beat.
> There are more scenes (than story beats) in a step outline.

Because scenes build upon one another in a logical progression, and sometimes it takes more than one scene to complete an important story beat (especially a pivotal story beat that moves the story forward exponentially), you must continually keep the difference between a story beat and a scene in mind in order to stay "on story." Remember that external and internal dramatic conflict creates the story beat.

By staying "on story," your *character-driven story beats* will offer the freedom to experiment with the scene-by-scene narrative of your step outline. Once you know the inner workings of the conflicts within your story, don't be afraid to brainstorm with original scenes that depict your story in exciting ways. In other words, commit to storytelling, develop the conflicts, and let the scenewriting begin!

With this approach, you will be willing (and delighted!) to throw out anything extraneous to the story. The first question to ask yourself is, "Where does my story begin?"

WHERE DOES MY STORY BEGIN?

The script begins with the opening sequence of shots that convey the essence of the story. However, the story begins with the main character's first moment of conflict conveyed by a scene or a few scenes that reveals the *story premise,* which is sometimes called the introduction to the story:

> In *Titanic,* the story begins with the underwater search for the ship and the discovery that a heart-shaped sapphire may lay among the wreckage. Rose (Kate Winslet), identifies herself as a survivor of the tragedy with a love story to tell.

> In *The Fugitive,* the story begins with the brutal murder of Dr. Kimble's wife (Sela Ward), and Dr. Kimble (Harrison Ford) being arrested for her murder.

> In *Tootsie,* the story begins with Michael (Dustin Hoffman) unable to get work as an actor, and unable to appreciate his birthday party hosted by his girl-friend (Teri Garr) of six years.

In film, the introduction to the story must begin as soon as possible, within the first few pages of the script. In step outline terms, this means sketching scenes that introduce the story concept clearly and concisely, as quickly as possible. If you begin by thinking in storytelling terms ("Once upon a time . . .") rather than plunging into locations and dialogue, you will move directly into depicting the main character and story concept.

The Steps of the Process

Create the Thirty-five to Forty-five Story Beats Have fun with the process of creating story beats. Create and experiment, shift ideas around, open up your mind to the infinite possibilities within the story.

Begin Thinking in "Set Pieces" The term *set piece* is very interesting. It originated in marketing departments, and until recently, it wasn't considered polite conversation among writers. The *set piece* originally referred to a scene in the movie that defined the story, requiring a big, expensive set, lots of production value, and sometimes hundreds of extras. Today, it has a much more significant meaning pertaining to marketing and storytelling. In current lingo, a *set piece* is much bigger than a story beat. It is a definitive screen moment that reveals the story concept in such a way that the marketing campaign can edit the scene into trailers and advertising and rely on word-of-mouth to bring in revenues. The pie-fornicating scene in *American Pie* is the quintessential "set piece." Mary's slicked-up hairdo in *There's Something About Mary* is a close second. In *Titanic,* it's the moment the ship spikes and descends into the water. In *Tootsie,* it's when the glamorized "Tootsie" struts in front of the United States flag. And in *The Fugitive,* it's when Dr. Kimble escapes the train wreck, becoming the fugitive on the run.

When marketing departments first coined the term *set piece,* they set the minimum standard of one per film. Since then, the minimum requirement has grown to five, with a recommended seven for today's market. Here is the current suggested "geography" for these seven set pieces:

- The opening of sequence one

- The protagonist-antagonist first scene in sequence three

- The antagonist's story thrust in sequence five

- The mid-point, favoring the protagonist

- The antagonist's triumph in sequence nine

- The protagonist's setback in sequence ten

- The climax and finale in sequence twelve

Develop story sequences based on spine This challenging task is where you apply your abstract and intuitive nature to your material as you are developing sequences that reflect what your story is about. It requires asking as many questions as possible pertaining to spine, whether your story is developed to its full potential, and then feeding the story sequences with subtle details that reflect the spine. At this juncture, it is crucial to keep in mind that each sequence has a "sequence climax" that builds toward the "story climax," and within these escalating climaxes, the story is inferred through the spine.

Create and sketch fifty to sixty scenes that reflect the spine, story beats, and sequences Finally, you are ready to work with creating dramatic conflict within scenes. The secret here is to understand the subconscious conflict within each scene first, then to understand and create the subtext of each scene as you create the subconscious dynamics and external conflict. Keep in mind that the location of the scene and the mechanics of the scene vary according to production requirements and financial restraints, but the subconscious conflict, external conflict, and subtext of the scene propel the story forward.

Evaluate story sequences in terms of spine Let story logic dominate by reminding yourself of the basics: What is the moral dilemma? How does it reveal the spine of the story? What is the climax of the story? What is the moral of the story? Are the scenes in proper story logic order?

Evaluate missing and extraneous elements of story Don't forget the structural basics for what's missing. What new characters can you create to reveal the subtle nuances of what your story is about? What existing characters, subplots, and extraneous elements do not serve the story and can be eliminated?

Create characterizations to solve problems Develop your thoughts and ideas into possible new characters that enhance your story. However, don't commit to them right out of the box. Remember, there are unlimited possibilities for characterization. Let your imagination run wild until you are satisfied that you have created the most story-worthy characters.

Use characterizations to solve problems Experiment with your new characters. Think through the plot and possible subplots to see if you can strengthen your story by integrating new or improved original characters into subplots that feed into the story.

Develop scenes into twelve story sequences using spine Go back to spine, and trust yourself. Think through the character-driven structural possibilities of subtext and dramatic conflict. Throw out or develop the scenes, based on whether they support or negate the spine of the story. Discover the beauty of the twelve-sequence story structure. It breaks down into a 3-6-3 format: There are three sequences to work with in the first act, six sequences in the second act, and three sequences in the third act. Above all, recognize that your story—*if it is completely original*—may not fit the paradigm exactly, but it should at least hit the basic story marks.

ACT II: INSIDE THE REAL STORY

The second act is where the main character enters the world where the story takes place. What really happens here—in the middle of the story—is that the main character is tested, challenged, confronted, and defeated during the rising action. This part of the story—Act II—is the body of the story. It is the *real story*. Act II is the most difficult portion to write because it reveals the main character's struggle and crisis, both internally and externally. In larger terms, it represents the struggle of the human condition.

Within the thirty-five to forty-five story beats, there are specific moments where the story moves forward exponentially rather than linearly. These primary story moments, which Syd Field defines as the Act One Plot Point, the Mid-Point, and the Act Two Plot Point, give primary definition to the second act. However, there are other important moments inside your story beats that give your story momentum:

Act II Complication

In addition to the story complication, there may be other complications, especially in Act II. An Act II complication is a heightened story beat that opposes the plot and does not pay off immediately. Rather, it stays with the main character as a challenge, and complicates the story as long as possible, hopefully throughout the entire story, until the climax and resolution.

Decoy

The decoy lures the audience into the trap of thinking the decoy is significant, usually as the villain or murderer or secondary love interest. The secret to creating a believable decoy is to develop an enticing character that sparks the audience's interest and leads them down the wrong path into a subplot that supports the story, but yields a resolution other than the audience imagines within the climax.

False Move

The false move makes the audience believe the main character is moving toward reaching his goal or mission, but in fact, the main character puts himself in further jeopardy. Action movies are filled with false moves, and so are comedies.

Foreshadowing

This is a literary concept used to describe how to set up thought-provoking clues about characters and subplots that are revealed as meaningful later in the story. The use of the word *foreshadowing* is usually reserved to describe something fundamental to understanding the depth of the story, such as *why the main character's fatal flaw gets in his or her way*, or *why the main character is going to be betrayed by a supporting character* at the end of the story.

Obstacle or Barrier

The obstacle or barrier gets in the way of the main character. It is something concrete that puts a temporary halt on the forward-moving action of the main character toward his goal or mission. Overcoming the obstacle or barrier either by moving in another direction or defeating it outright, the main character continues to move forward toward achieving his goal or mission.

Reveal

Revelation or reveal is one of the most important concepts in storytelling, continually evaluated by writers, directors, producers, and executives in various ways during the screenwriting process: *What is the reveal? When is it revealed? How is it revealed? Who reveals it?* The *reveal* is a plot point or character moment that is made known to the audience at a specific time relative to the progression of the plot and the dramatic insights of the story. Whatever is revealed—something from the past, a clue to the murderer, the location where a murder took place, the state of mind of a character—has always existed within the story. However, *when the story element is revealed, and how it is revealed*, must be significant to the progression of the story and contribute to the meaning and depth of the story.

Reversal

The reversal is a story barrier where the main character reaches a point where the only move he or she can make is in the opposite direction of his or her goal. This is a substantial character-driven story event wherein the main character makes a momentous decision, such as the family man surrendering to adultery, the philanderer committing to his marriage, the alcoholic accepting he or she is powerless to alcohol, or the coward deciding to risk his life for others. The reversal loads the emotional weight of the story with a powerful contradiction.

Set-up and Payoff

The set-up usually refers to the first fifteen pages of the script, which lay out the basics of the main character's situation. However, throughout the script, we set up all sorts of characters, clues, story points, plot moments, dialogue, and visual images that pay off throughout the script with a particular meaning that advances the understanding and depth of the story.

Surprise

Surprises are rare, because it's so difficult to execute a *surprise* successfully, which is why audiences love them. Whether it's a surprise revealed through a villain, a surprise entrance from a comedian, a surprise seduction that turns deadly, or a stream of surprises at the climax that burst into a surprise ending, the audience lives for surprises! In fact, a movie filled with surprises guarantees word-of-mouth raves that will pack the theaters and break the box office.

ACT III: BUILDING TOWARD A CLIMAX

Act III looks easy because you only need to write twenty-five more pages. But starting the third act can be a difficult transition, not because of scenewriting or where the story is going, rather because you must understand the internal conflict of the main character and why he must turn his or her back on the mission or goal for the first time. This requires figuring out how to depict his or her internal motivation and how it has evolved by being tested with overwhelming challenges. The secret here is to work from inside the main character's state of mind to recover his motivation and renew his moral strength to achieve the external goal of the story.

···

Act III begins with depicting the main character's internal desire to recover motivation and renew his moral strength to achieve the external goal of the story.

···

Many screenplays go off-story at this juncture, favoring action sequences over deepening the moral strength of the main character. While action may seem exciting and original in presentation, it actually interrupts the audience's ability to come to terms with the main character's renewed motivation and resurrected mission or goal, which become the basis for his or her final transformation that occurs in Act III of the story.

The Setback

The *setback* is one of the most interesting and exciting dramatic moments in the third act. Now that the main character is back on track, moving forward toward achieving the goal or mission, the best story move is to sock it to him once again, this time with a setback and big set piece that is an even more devastating defeat than previous ones.

Rising from the Ashes

Finally, by testing the main character to the limit, the main character *rises from the ashes* of the setback, and springs forward morally, ready to take on the antagonist and anyone else who stands in his way. The secret here is to reorient the goal or mission for the audience in moral terms, and put the momentum of the story into full gear.

The Climax

The main character's epiphany or moment of realization features his newly discovered insight pertaining to his character growth. The secret is to feature his flaw, which was set up in the opening of the story, tested in Act II, and by now has been internally resolved. At the climax, the main character is morally fortified: He is willing and able to confront, overcome, or defeat the antagonist.

The Ending

The ending, or resolution, occurs in the last five pages of the script. You have only a few pages to tie up the loose ends of the story here, so take your time writing the ending. Create a big, exciting set piece at the finish of your action story, or a suspenseful final reveal in your thriller, or hilarious character regression in your comedy. In any case, this is your chance to give the audience a big send-off so they exit the theater recommending your film to everyone they know.

THE PROFESSIONAL OUTLINE

When you write a step outline for yourself, it is a blueprint for your eyes only. You can make it as long as possible or as short as possible to lay out exactly what you need in terms of story, character, and spine requirements.

As a professional, however, if you are asked to hand in a step outline as part of a "step deal," then you must practice industry standards not only for your professional reputation, but for the practical matter of getting paid.

....

*A step deal means you get paid for each step you render
as a writer-for-hire:
step outline, first draft, two rewrites, and a polish.*

....

Although a step deal may sound good, the studio and producers reserve the right to cut off the writer's service at each and every level of the deal. After the first story meeting with producers and executives, if the story is approved, the step outline is the first written document of a step deal.

In a step outline, tell the story in prose, scene by scene, in twenty to forty pages.

The professional step outline tells the story in prose, as if the reader has never heard it before. The acceptable step outline for payment purposes would be anywhere from twenty pages to forty pages, and if you are writing a television movie or mini-series, keep in mind that television requirements are often more stringent than feature film requirements. The practical reason for this standard exercise is quite simple: You must be able to tell the story clearly and concisely for those executives whom you have not met, but who authorize your paycheck. They need to see your step outline to know that your work has been accepted by producers and executives.

Ironically, few movies actually resemble the writer's original step outline, but putting that aside, the step outline is the first place where you can experiment with story, make mistakes, and get the feedback you need to proceed to the next level. It's also an opportunity to create exciting set pieces that define the story. In fact, as you begin to respect the rigor of the process, you will find that creating the step outline is similar to drawing up the architectural plans for a home. Once you finally break ground and begin construction, your screenplay will have a life of its own!

CHAPTER NINETEEN

Creating the Scene

A scene conveys a *story beat* or *story point,* through a concrete dramatic scenario that expresses dramatic conflict on several levels, including scene elements such as location, time setting, character or characters, visual images, theme, and subtext.

The secret to creating a great scene is to understand the unconscious (internal) conflict of the main character within the scene as well as the conscious (external) character conflict, and to know how these conflicts advance the story, reveal character, portray a theme, and can be portrayed as an image.

PREPARING THE SCENE

In preparation for creating the scene, you must think through some basic ideas of what you plan to accomplish dramatically and in story terms before you begin. This is a process of setting objectives within the scene: a *primary objective* that pertains to the *story beat* and *conflict(s)* you wish to portray to move the story forward, and *secondary objectives* that pertain to the finer points of the scene, such as what you plan to reveal and how you plan to reveal it, either through characterization or through images and sounds.

DEFINING THE CONFLICT

The most difficult part of creating the scene is understanding your story well enough to know the progression of story beats and *understanding the unconscious and conscious conflict at work within the story.* First, you must understand the overall or central conflict of the story; then you can define the development of the story beats through conflict in every scene and every sequence. Now, as you have worked through these multiple conflicts *as story beats* into scenes, the challenge is to return to each scene, and redefine the levels of conflict so that you can add the various levels of expression such as irony, hyperbole, or paradox into your scenes.

CHARACTERS AS IDEAS

Once you have placed the story beats into *storytelling sequences* of the step outline and redefined the unconscious and conscious conflicts of the main character, then the process becomes analytical. You must decide which characters are necessary to create the levels of conflict *within each scene* to advance the story. The potential trap here is to portray plot movement by explaining the scene with expository dialogue, without any unconscious insight or subtext. Take your time. If you find yourself sketching dialogue, take a break and determine what you are trying to achieve *through the story beat*. Then, try to achieve it through characterization, action, and images.

CREATING THE ACTION

Actors act, they don't tell. And they act with attitude. You have decided which character or characters you need to create the scene, and now you must give them *action in the form of deeds and behavior* to tell the story.

- **Deeds and behavior** *Deeds* are what the character does to advance the plot and story. Deeds are related to outer story goals of the characters. *Behavior,* in contrast, reveals the inner nature and inner conflict of the characters. Behavior is unique to each character.

....

Deeds are external. Behavior is unique to each character.

....

- **Conceptualizing action** Conceptualizing the action of the scene requires weaving together conflict and plot. This is a process that requires synthesizing the multiple objectives of the scene into a dynamic beginning, middle, and end, with a climax and resolution that pushes the story forward.

LOCATIONS

Although the location of a scene can be extremely important in production terms, in storytelling terms, the location can sometimes be inconsequential. By reminder, the elements of story (character, state-of-mind, premise, situation, story complication, etc.) are essential to storytelling. As the writer, it is within your domain to create and eliminate locations in the script, based on whether they contribute to the story. If your story requires glamorous and/or original locations to convey the story, then go for it—create set pieces that feature these locations in a big way!

STAGING

Staging refers to how to *get into the scene* and how to *get out of the scene*. Staging also reveals how each element of the scene is dramatically presented and in what order. Although staging is specifically the work of the director, it is important to know, as the writer, that there is always a more efficient way to stage the dramatic reveals within a scene in the most compelling way. When a reader comments, "It's an easy read," they usually mean the staging of the story is presented clearly so it is easy to understand the story from scene to scene.

CREATING DIALOGUE AND MONOLOGUES

The on-screen spoken words between and among characters are called *dialogue,* whereas a *monologue* is a speech delivered by one character.

In the early days of silent film, dialogue and monologues did not exist. Filmmakers moved into the era of "talkies" in the late 1920s, and gradually dialogue became an important storytelling element in moviemaking. Today, the use of dialogue varies from genre to genre, sometimes as the primary storytelling tool, and other times, displaced by visuals that tell the story with as little dialogue as possible. Here is an excellent framework from which you can appreciate how to use dialogue in your work:

Dialogue is the thing!

This is the type of movie where the story is revealed as if it were a theatrical play rather than a movie. It is not inferior or superior; it is merely presented in such a way that the dominant storytelling element is dialogue. *Amadeus, Shakespeare In Love, Sleuth, When Harry Met Sally, A Few Good Men,* and *Lawrence Of Arabia* are vivid examples of dialogue-driven films.

Naturalistic

This dialogue exquisitely portrays the characters and their milieu. In fact, the movie depicts the vernacular of its characters so intricately and accurately that the screenplay appears to be seamless. *On the Waterfront, Casino, Raging Bull,* and *Bull Durham,* through the use of naturalistic dialogue, capture the ambiance of the story as well as the ethnic origin and cultural specificity of their characters.

Visualistic

Some movies rely primarily on visuals rather than dialogue to tell the story. *Bullitt* is an example of a movie with extremely minimalist dialogue, whereas *Snatch, Matrix, Moulin Rouge, Bladerunner, Crimson Tide, Black Rain, Black Hawk Down,* and the *Batman* films are primarily visualistic, but also convey their stories through dialogue.

Another warning about "expository dialogue": Using *expository dialogue to set forth the literal meaning or expressed purpose of the scene* is deadly. If you find yourself "staging" scenes with people talking to one another, or making confessions to one another, you are headed in the wrong direction.

Expository dialogue is the ultimate no-no!

Most interesting characters are reluctant to reveal important information in dialogue at all. They typically keep a secret or two, even from their love interest. By exercising the discipline of keeping a few "character secrets" to yourself, you can create and reveal on-screen complexities of characterization.

CREATING A CLIMAX

My students, clients, and fellow writers respond with groans of exhaustion when I remind them that every scene has a climax, every sequence has a climax, every story has a climax, and that they all build upon one another. But that doesn't stop me from continually challenging them to develop scene climaxes and sequence climaxes that progress toward the *story climax*. The secret here is that each climax is built on three beats: establishing the conflict, developing the rising action, and building toward the moment of climax between the two forces of conflict.

CREATING A STORY PIVOT AND TRANSITION

In movies, each scene is part of a series of scenes in a sequence, and each scene links to the next scene by "story logic" in an order that makes "story sense." The link between each scene is a *pivot, on which the story turns.* The story pivots move the story forward in a vital way, scene by scene, toward a climax of each sequence that in turn moves forward to the next sequence. After each scene is written, and after each sequence is completed, the process is not complete until the "story pivot" is created, requiring a bridge or *transition,* to the next scene or sequence. Most transitions occur with a visual image, but sometimes a sound cue can be more effective, as in the Academy Award–winning movie *Amadeus,* which integrates the music of Mozart throughout, conveying the tragic demise of Antonio Salieri (F. Murray Abraham) in operatic terms, with sound and visual transitions.

PERSONIFYING THE MAIN CHARACTER'S CENTRAL CONFLICT

Our most memorable scenes personify the central conflict of the story through the internal conflict of the main character, with powerful images and external conflict:

- *Titanic:* Jack (Leonard DiCaprio) risks his life to save the third-class passengers, and Rose (Kate Winslet) joins him, rejecting her social position, which would have guaranteed her a place on one of the rescue boats. The audience is completely immersed in the central conflict: Jack breaks open the door to steerage, the water rushes forth, freeing the third-class passengers, and we experience the dramatic essence of the story. Jack, the classic hero, personifies his willingness to sacrifice his life for others, and in so doing, earns eternal devotion from his beloved Rose.

- *Tootsie:* After Michael (Dustin Hoffman) wins the audition for the role of Emily Kimberly on the soap opera *Southwest General,* he is fascinated by his girlfriend Sandy's (Teri Garr) wardrobe. He enjoys trying on a couple dresses, admires himself in the mirror, and starts to slip off his pants—only to be discovered by Sandy, who pertly asks him if he's gay. His pants fall to his ankles. He opens his arms to Sandy mock romantically, declares his undying love for her, and ends up sleeping with her to prove he's straight. At that moment, Michael personifies the central conflict: He is a man pretending to be a woman who is pretending to be a man. Disgusted with himself, he attaches to Dorothy's persona to correct his flaws, and ends up becoming a better man.

- *The Fugitive:* Gerard (Tommy Lee Jones) chases Kimble (Harrison Ford) to the sewage tunnels, which lead to a dramatic precipice with a waterfall. As they confront each other, Kimble points a gun on Gerard, and asserts his innocence: "I did not kill my wife." Gerard, who half-believes Kimble for one moment, retorts enigmatically: "I don't care." Lurking inside this moment, Gerard is mystified by the fact that Kimble, a convicted murderer, would spare the life of his would-be captor. As Kimble leaps into the waterfall, he personifies the central conflict: He becomes a fugitive from injustice, consistently extending his hand to others as he doggedly uncovers the mysterious circumstances surrounding his wife's murder.

SCENE WRITERS BEWARE!

Creating the scene is an intricate process, which can only be accomplished if the overall conflict, story logic, story beats, story pivots, and story sequences are in place. If you find yourself writing scenes before these elements are worked out, then you are merely sketching ideas *as a scenewriter* to explore possibilities of the narrative or plot. This may help you discover conflict and story logic, but there is no substitute for knowing how to personify the central conflict of the story.

CHAPTER TWENTY

Originality

GREAT stories give us a strong feeling of personal identification with the characters, especially the main character. Great movies provoke a powerful unconscious emotional response to the story that we have never felt before. The combination of what we see and hear on-screen affects us psychologically and communally in ways that we cannot possibly predict. How we accomplish this abstract task as storytellers is recognized as *originality*.

· ·

Inventive screenwriters express originality.
Originality is achieved through tone, point of view, and symbolism.

· ·

TONE: YOUR UNIQUE VOICE

Tone refers to the *frame of mind* or *state-of-mind* of the story itself, what the storyteller conveys through the pitch, accents, and intonation of the storyteller's voice. Very few writers begin with a specific tone, and yet, tone represents the unique voice behind your story—*your voice as a storyteller*—that which distinguishes a screenplay written by you, as opposed to a screenplay written by any other writer.

In fact, when your agent, producer, colleagues, or script consultant suggests that the tone of your script is not clear, or that the tone varies from scene to scene, it means that you haven't excavated the events of the material deeply enough and given over your personal voice and insight to the story in order to discover the tonal possibilities within the material. Tone—the voice of the storyteller—is a refined artistic element that has enhanced these outstanding films:

- *Being John Malkovich* This wonderful little movie, written by Charlie Kaufman, directed by Spike Jonze, starring John Cusack, reveals the whimsical universe of Craig Schwartz, an unemployed puppeteer who maintains a menagerie of animals in a small apartment that he shares with his dowdy wife Lotte (Cameron Diaz). Like Alice in *Through the Looking-Glass,* Craig discovers a passageway that leads him into an extraordinary world where he enters the mind of actor John Malkovich for roughly fifteen minutes at a time, after which he is ejected onto the New Jersey Turnpike. During each fifteen minutes, however, he is able to understand the mysteries of the John Malkovich's unconscious as well as the complexities of both genders, male and female. Through Craig Schwartz's experiences, Charlie Kaufman uses his marvelous voice and unique tone to create one of the most original screenplays ever written.

- *Psycho* Alfred Hitchcock's classic psychological suspense thriller presents the story of Marion Crane (Janet Leigh), an attractive woman who embezzles cash from her boss to assist her married lover in divorcing his wife. She enters the psychotic, fragile world of Nor-

man Bates (Anthony Perkins), an emotionally stunted motel propri-
etor who is obsessed by his domineering, invalid mother. Unable to
make man-to-woman contact with the sexually provocative Miss
Crane, Bates brutally kills her by stabbing her to death in perhaps
the most memorable shower scene in the history of film.

• *Sunset Boulevard* Another classic, this is the story of aging silent
film queen Norma Desmond (Gloria Swanson) who refuses to believe that her time in the spotlight is over. The story opens with a
bullet-riddled body of a man floating facedown in Desmond's swimming pool. The story flashes back to tell the story of how a hack
screenwriter named Joe Gillis (William Holden) ended up dead in
her pool. His accidental meeting with Desmond plunges the penni-
less Gillis into a moral and social conundrum. He desperately needs
the pipe dream job she offers him of rewriting a script she hopes to
launch as her comeback vehicle, but by accepting her proposition,
he becomes a virtual prisoner and kept man. His attempt to break
free from her strange, narcissistic world costs him his life.

• *American Beauty* This comic-tragedy about an American family
is filled with hilarious dark moments between Lester Burnham
(Kevin Spacey) and his wife, Carolyn (Annette Bening). This quirky
story portrays a middle-aged man who is emotionally estranged
from his wife, and who alienates his teenage daughter (Thora Birch)
by lusting after her best friend, Angela (Mena Suvari). His conscience is overwhelmed with lechery in a disturbingly realistic way,
and despite the black comedic tone that seeks to lighten Lester's
journey, his tragic ending at the hand of his neighbor, a latently ho-
mosexual marine (Chris Cooper), leaves us with a dark, almost
pitch-black story conclusion.

• *Men In Black* Who can forget the hilariously inventive tone of this
Barry Sonnenfeld film about two FBI agents who are engaged in a secret struggle against aliens bent on destroying Earth? What makes
this work, and what makes all of Barry Sonnenfeld's movies (*Get
Shorty, Men in Black II*) so endearing to mainstream audiences is his

original voice and comedic genius, which translates into an over-the-top outrageous tone that keeps us laughing from beginning to end.

• *Tootsie* This Academy Award–winning screenplay by Murray Schisgal and Larry Gelbart is extremely well crafted, but what makes this film so successful with audiences is its light tone, which is consistently delivered through gender irony and human paradox. Dustin Hoffman captures his male ego as Michael Dorsey and his female alter ego as Dorothy Michaels with outrageous intensity and flair. Director Sydney Pollack delivers the one-two satiric punch over and over again, earning *Tootsie* the position as the number 2 all-time favorite comedy, according to the American Film Institute.

• *Some Like It Hot* Billy Wilder and I.A.L. Diamond collaborated as writers to spoof gangster movies from the 1930s in this classic film, which according to the American Film Institute, is considered the number 1 all-time favorite comedy. Two out-of-work Depression-era jazz musicians, Joe (Tony Curtis) and Jerry (Jack Lemmon), accidentally witness the St. Valentine's Day Massacre. Forced to leave town, Joe and Jerry dress up as women, and join Sweet Sue's all-girl band, as Josephine and Daphne. Joe/Josephine is thrown for a loop when he meets the sexy, adorable Sugar Kane (Marilyn Monroe) while Jerry/Daphne catches the eye of a wealthy lovesick tycoon named Osgood E. Fielding III (Joe E. Brown). All pull together to create a memorable comedy that maintains its comedic tone from beginning to end.

POINT OF VIEW: THE A-LIST DECISION

The point-of-view decision also expresses originality. The point-of-view character represents your own unique voice within the story. By creating a unique and vital character that interacts with the main character, you, as the writer, have the opportunity to reveal the inner struggle of the main character through your own insight.

Choosing and developing the point-of-view character is not a static endeavor. It is a decision that is dynamic, arising after thoughtful consideration and experimentation, sometimes during or after the first draft of the screenplay. Clients and students often ask if the main character can also be the point-of-view character. In literature, the answer is yes. In film, the answer is no, not for the screen. The audience needs to identify with an on-screen character who gives the audience continual understanding and insight about the inner struggle of the main character. Some of the most memorable characters in the history of cinema are point-of-view characters:

• *Casablanca* Rick's (Humphrey Bogart) background as a true antihero and his moral dilemma regarding whether to choose his romance with Ilsa (Ingrid Bergman) or to aid the French Resistance for the liberty and freedom of the world are cleverly and thoughtfully dramatized through sparkling conflict with Renault, the Prefet de Police (Claude Rains).

• *Gone With the Wind* Scarlett O'Hara's (Vivien Leigh) vanity, loves, and losses are expertly revealed by contrast with the lovely, generous, and forgiving Melanie (Olivia DeHavilland), who represents the refinement of the South, and teaches us to genuinely love one another despite betrayals, losses, and disappointments.

• *Chicago* Roxie Hart's (Renee Zellweger) wily Machiavellian plot to literally get away with murder is hilariously depicted by her clever faux-innocent persona in contrast with the delectable, in-your-face Velma Kelly (Catherine Zeta-Jones), who sets the darkly comedic tone of the story through her point of view.

• *American Beauty* Lester Burnham's (Kevin Spacey) fall from grace and descent into lust is remarked literally by his daughter's next-door friend, Ricky Fitts (Wes Bentley), who uses his camera to reveal a skewered look at the Burnham family through the next-door window.

• *Beauty and the Beast* The selfish, unkind Beast must earn the love and respect of the generous and virtuous Belle who, by her loyalty and kindness, helps us understand his struggle to let go of his beastly ways in order to recover his identity and stature as a prince.

SYMBOLISM: THE VISUAL ART FORM

Symbolism is the art of using objects or actions to represent a repressed complex meaning through unconscious associations. Using symbolism to create imagery throughout your screenplay is one of the most advanced elements of storytelling. Few writers and directors actually reach this level of accomplishment, but James Cameron, Steven Spielberg, and Milos Forman have succeeded at the highest level in these memorable films.

• *Titanic* The *Titanic* represents the unsinkable hopes and dreams of humanity. Watching this magnificent ship leave port is one of the most exciting visuals in all of filmmaking because we know that the R.M.S. *Titanic* will encounter the fateful iceberg and sink. Watching the passengers struggle for life as the ship spikes and goes down takes us into a harrowing journey.

There are other memorable symbols that James Cameron uses beautifully throughout this epic movie, which features a powerful theme and surpasses all other films as the most appealing commercial film ever made:

  ◆ The heart-shaped blue sapphire that symbolizes Rose (Kate Winslet) and Jack's (Leonardo DiCaprio) eternal love for each other.
  ◆ The image of the Architect (Victor Garber) of *Titanic* watching the ticking timepiece on the fireplace mantel as the ship goes down symbolizes man's arrogance in assuming the indestructible nature of one of his creations.
  ◆ Rose and Jack's frenzied Irish jig represents letting go of the social and class differences that keep these young lovers apart.

• *Schindler's List* The opening sequence portrays Oskar Schindler (Liam Neeson), a Nazi obsessed by vanity, material possessions, and money. He is a man with no capacity for shame or remorse, a man who seeks to exploit Jews for his own financial advantage. The symbol that dominates this magnificent movie, which is shot in black and white, is the image an innocent little girl whom Schindler nicknames "Red Coat" as he travels throughout Krakow, and whose red coat Spielberg portrays as the only color image in the movie. When Schindler sees "Red Coat" atop a pile of dead bodies, carted through the streets of Krakow to be disposed of by incineration, Schindler is forced to confront the inhumanity and atrocities of the Nazi regime and challenges himself to change his personal ways, by making the momentous decision to spare the lives of the Jews around him.

There are many other powerful symbols that screenwriter Steven Zaillian and director Steven Spielberg use throughout *Schindler's List,* which won seven Academy Awards, including Best Picture:

◆ Christian images (of a religion that Oskar Schindler has long since abandoned) become the outward signs by which he gradually comes to integrate his newfound respect for his fellow man and his desire to mend his womanizing ways so he can reconcile with his beloved wife.

◆ The list itself, typed by Schindler's accountant Itzhak Stern (Ben Kingsley), includes 147 names, represents the enormity of Schindler's accomplishment, yet at the same time serves to fuel his regret at not being able to save one more life.

◆ Schindler's material possessions represent his vanity and corruption. They become increasingly meaningless to him as he gradually adopts a moral compass that elevates him to a man worthy of our admiration and affection.

• *Amadeus* The story of Antonio Salieri (F. Murray Abraham) and his archnemesis Wolfgang Amadeus Mozart (Tom Hulce), written by Peter Schaefer and directed by Milos Forman, is filled with the musical genius of Mozart and flows with Christian symbolism. Court composer and mediocre musician, Salieri is a pseudo-religious man who is driven by his envy of the musically gifted Mozart (whose middle name, Amadeus, means "the soul of God"). By seeking to destroy Mozart, Salieri, in fact, destroys himself. Rather than experiencing remorse and begging forgiveness during confession to a young amiable priest, Salieri is strangely proud of what he believes is his greatest desire—that is, to destroy Mozart. Unwilling to accept absolution for his envy, Salieri self-destructs at the end of the story.

Other powerful symbols, which director Milos Forman uses throughout this magnificent film that won eight Academy Awards, include:

* Operatic touches, such as *The Marriage Of Figaro, The Magic Flute,* and Mozart's *Requiem.*
* Mozart's father represents the nurturing father figure Salieri has never had. Salieri assumes Mozart's father's identity posthumously—dressed as a dark, forbidding ghost—to gradually drive Mozart insane.
* The pieces of gold paid to Mozart by Salieri for writing the *Requiem* represent the irony of Mozart's selling the "soul of god" to the one who most wants to destroy him.

Understanding the internal conflict of the main character is the key to understanding the unconscious level of the story and expressing originality with your own unique voice. There are many ways to achieve this through state-of-mind and characterization, but developing tone, point of view, and symbolism deepen the story and creates memorable screen moments, sometimes subtle and refined, other times bold and imaginative. Applying advanced storytelling techniques requires artistic restraint, akin to using a paintbrush during the final touch-up of an oil painting. You may know what you want in the final effect, but it requires imagination and thoughtful consideration to make these choices sparingly to express maximum effect.

CHAPTER TWENTY-ONE

Where Good Scripts
Go Wrong

PULLING together all the essential elements of a screenplay can be very challenging. There are a number of junctures at which a screenplay can take a turn for the worse. In my experience, there are four categories where scripts can go wrong. The first includes common story mistakes from which you can recover by redirecting the story. The second involves storytelling traps, where the story reaches a dead end before it begins. The third are missteps that become land mines where the story implodes upon itself, never to be recovered. The fourth are technical errors that make it impossible to read or interpret what is happening in the script.

COMMON STORY MISTAKES

By far, the biggest project killer is not being able to adequately answer: *Where does the story begin?* Usually there are a number of problems connected to this basic issue.

Introducing the Story

A great script usually begins with an exciting opening series of shots that convey the essence of the story. However, the story itself begins with the main character's first major *moment of conflict*, which reveals the *story premise*. This moment of conflict is also called the *inciting incident*, a term that originates with Aristotle, the ancient Greek philosopher-dramatist, and has been popularized by Robert McKee in his book *Story*. Regardless of terminology, introducing the story *of a screenplay* must occur within the first few pages of the script.

One of the most deadly screenwriting habits is the tendency to meander through the first twenty or thirty pages of the script, delaying the story premise until page thirty! It is essential that storytellers know what the story is, where it begins, and by using conflict, introduce it as soon as possible. If you think "Once upon a time . . ." as you begin, you will naturally move straight into your story through your main character's internal and external conflict.

Inner world and inner conflict

The inner world—or state-of-mind—of the main character is another area of difficulty, even for experienced writers. This is where story insight takes place. If state-of-mind of the main character is not properly established, the audience cannot participate in the story, let alone in the external events the main character faces. Paradoxically, the inner or unconscious conflicts of the main character remain constant throughout the story as he or she confronts outer conflicts and overcomes the external challenges of the goal or mission. This contradiction is both the beauty and the curse of human nature.

This "dual dynamic" is the basis of creating and developing the main character's insight pertaining to what he has experienced throughout the story. In other words, although the story takes place in an exciting, ever-changing external world through the *actions of the main character*, the abstract understanding of the story is filtered through the main character's *constant inner conflict*.

Missing story elements

Although most screenwriters begin with a great idea and an exciting main character with a strong motivation, their stories often derail because story elements are missing. Developing a moral dilemma for the main character is the cornerstone of the dramatic situation. Even a formidable antagonist and strong plot cannot make up for this missing element, because there is no inner story for the audience to follow. Another element that gets short shrift is the story complication. The story complication keeps the conflict and momentum of the story going throughout the second act. Its absence is usually connected to an insufficiently developed antagonist.

Missing story points

The main character drives the plot and the story. The major twelve story beats, or story points, reveal the emotional story, which we experience by identifying with the main character. They are highlighted through the central conflict—internal and external—between the main character and the antagonist. Supporting characters and subplots feed into the main plot and story, giving it depth. When story points are missing, the underlying cause is insufficient development of the forces of antagonism.

Building toward the climax

Unnecessary scenes and false steps that do not support the inner story—or emotional story—get in the way of audiences enjoying and experiencing the main character's journey. Conversely, inviting the audience to attach to the emotional story opens up all sorts of possibilities within the external plot, goal, and mission of the story. Letting go of superfluous scenes and dialogue allows the emotional story to shine, which increases momentum toward the story climax.

Using antagonists to create a "star vehicle"

Screenwriters rarely give enough story to the antagonist, yet the most memorable screenplays (*Lawrence of Arabia, Schindler's List, Amadeus*) feature tremendous antagonists and forces of antagonism. The common tendency is to under-write the antagonist and miss opportunities to develop the opposing elements of the plot and story. The ability to create a completely original main character is a great gift, but the challenge is to create an antagonist who is equal and opposing to the main character. Intense conflict between two opposing forces is what elevates the appeal of the main character for the audience. This is known as creating a "star vehicle." A star vehicle is a project with "major star appeal," and it becomes an A-list screenplay when it attracts an A-list actor, director, or production company.

STORYTELLING TRAPS

Traps are seductive. You think you are headed in the right direction. You think you have discovered gold, and all of a sudden you are slowly sinking in quicksand. You have mistaken story elements from storytelling techniques.

Back-story

Back-story refers to the personal history of the main character, but also includes the events of the narrative that have occurred before the story begins. Each supporting character also has a personal history that is part of the back-story, which includes the following elements, most of which has *happened off-screen*, before the story begins.

- The immediate past of the main character
- The long-term past of the main character

- The immediate and long-term past of the antagonist(s)

- The immediate and long-term pasts of all supporting characters

- The events of the narrative that occurred prior to this story

....

Back-story happens off-screen, before the story begins.

....

The potential trap occurs when back-story is featured on screen as if it is part of the story. The preferred approach is to abbreviate the back-story using storytelling techniques. Telescope back-story thematically, reducing it to its simplest meaning and form. Reveal it gradually by inference—through forward-moving story events and plot points as the story unfolds—but only if it helps the audience to understand the meaning of the story.

Keep in mind that we all have a back-story wherever we go, no matter what we are doing. Yet few of us make a reference to it, unless specific past events apply to the present task at hand. If we do refer to back-story events, we do so because they have a specific connection to the present.

Flashbacks and flash-cuts

In some stories, *flashbacks* and *flash-cuts* are used to reveal the story. These are storytelling devices that differ from back-story in that they are *techniques* used to reveal the forward-moving story. The general rule is that if specific information (or conflict) from the main character's past is necessary to the forward-moving action of the story, then it becomes part of story and is revealed as a story beat, through a flashback or flash-cut. Again, the prevailing criterion is whether the conflict or incident merits a story beat. Storytelling devices support the story, not the other way around.

• A *flashback* is an extended series of shots which conveys an important and meaningful story point.

• A *flash-cut* is a screenwriting transition that is quick and subliminal, often revealing a psychological element pertaining to the main character's state of mind, and sometimes revealing a quick plot point or story point.

....

Flashbacks and flash-cuts may seem like back-story.
However, because they actually move story forward, they are
considered part of the story.

....

Titanic is told in "bookends," which are a particular type of flashback that frame the story, one that opens the story and another that help us understand the story at the end. *Titanic* also employs a memorable flash-cut at the climax of the story when young Rose DeWitt Bukater (Kate Winslet) and Jack Dawson (Leonard DiCaprio) fill the screen with their romantic kiss, startling us with the memory of their enduring romantic love through the point of view of mature Rose Calvert (Gloria Stewart).

Tootsie opens with a stylish comic sequence that features flash-cuts from Michael Dorsey's (Dustin Hoffman) immediate past as representative of his state of mind. With his internal conflict firmly in place, the premise of the story moves forward briskly without flashbacks and flash-cuts.

The opening sequence of *The Fugitive* employs compelling flash-cuts of Richard Kimble (Harrison Ford) and his wife (Sela Ward) that are intercut with her murder, without revealing the one-armed man. This sets the stage for his wrongful conviction, but also sets the stage for effective flash-cuts throughout the film featuring Kimble as he leads Officer Gerard (Tommy Lee Jones) to uncover the details of the sinister plot behind the one-armed man.

Expository dialogue

If actions speak louder than words, then dialogue does not—and cannot—tell a story. Dramatic conflict, unconscious conflict, and dramatic subtext are revealed as inner workings of the emotional story. Dialogue, however, is only representational of what a character says, reflecting these deeper meanings. Although dialogue is considered important to great screenwriting, less is more. Using dialogue to expose the story—expository dialogue—is a trap. It seems easy. It seems seductive. It brings the story to a halt because it is dreadful to watch.

LAND MINES WHERE THE STORY IMPLODES

Killing off the movie star

Creating a great character—especially the leading character—for a major movie star is useless if you kill off the character early in the story. You are not just killing off a character, you are killing off the movie star. This infuriates readers who are looking for movies that audiences want to see, so your script won't even be read, let alone make it to the screen. In order to attract a movie star, the rule of thumb is that the leading character should be on-screen 97 percent of the time. During the other 3 percent, the on-screen characters should be talking about him.

Good vs. Evil

Values go clockwise, not the other way around. In storytelling, this means that mass audiences follow stories in simple terms—good vs. evil. They are attracted to lasting themes that draw on traditional values that are universal and familiar. In fact, they feel shortchanged if there are moral ambiguities throughout your story. Human nature gravitates toward stories that affirm our deepest core values about "life, liberty, and the pursuit of happiness." In practical story terms, this means that there must be a point of reference among the characters you portray that represents what is right and just—what is commonly recognized as goodness. Regardless what story you tell—even the most gruesome murder story—mainstream audiences cannot tolerate exploitation of defenseless and vulnerable human beings on-screen. This includes movies that portray harm to babies, children, animals, elderly, the infirmed, the helpless, and the unborn. While horrifying things happen in life, it's up to the storyteller to understand how to treat gruesome realities and evil deeds on-screen. If you carelessly mishandle this basic trust with your audience, they may never forgive you.

Silence of the Lambs is an excellent example of a story where goodness triumphs over evil, without exploiting the defenseless. Clarice (Jodie Foster) comes to terms with her painful past through compelling, but troubling mind games with the perverse Hannibal Lecter (Anthony Hopkins), who provokes our curiosity by his obsession with cannibalism, without our being subjected to the off-screen gruesome deeds of the tattooed serial killer who skins people alive.

Limited thinking

Another deadly mistake is limiting your thinking. There is no substitute for consistently reconsidering and rethinking the elements of your story. As earlier stated, the suggested approach is to work with the main character by developing antagonistic forces through opposing ideas. By examining and questioning the interplay of ideas and how they are affected by conflict, you allow yourself an open-ended state of mind that will give you the confidence to discover new possibilities within your story on a daily basis.

TECHNICAL CONFUSION

Technical confusion accounts for a great number of screenplays that are rejected. There is only one format and one font. Also, it is important to differentiate between creative story elements and technical elements of screenwriting.

Format and font

Format and font are "Standard U.S.," approximately 100–120 pages, typed in 12 pt. Courier, and bound with three brass fasteners and card-stock covers. If you do not meet the industry standard, nobody will read your script, not even in a classroom setting. The two most popular screenwriting programs, Final Draft and Movie Magic Screenwriter, will prevent you from making errors in format and font. Also, there are websites where you can download shooting scripts from major motion pictures such as *American Beauty, The Sixth Sense,* and *Almost Famous.* To become familiar with "Standard U.S. Format," see Appendix D and visit these websites:

- Simply Scripts: www.simplyscripts.com

- Script Crawler: www.scriptcrawler.com

- Internet Script Database: www.iscriptdb.com

- Drew's Script-o-Rama: www.script-o-rama.com

Elements of screenwriting

The *elements of screenwriting* are technical script requirements that you actually see on the written page. *Transitions* represent pivots within the story. They tell us when the story begins and where it's going with sound and visual clues.

FADE IN:

CUT TO:

INTER-CUT:

FLASH-CUT:

FADE TO BLACK.

FADE UP:

DISSOLVE TO:

FADE OUT.

Slug lines tell us where and when the scene takes place. *Scene descriptions* tell us the action of the scene and any other images or sounds pertinent to the scene.

> EXT. BEVERLY HILLS—CHIC OFFICE—DAY
>
> Two screenwriters, JOE and JANE exit. A champagne-colored Jaguar glistens in the sunlight. Joe and Jane could never be happier.

Characters and *dialogue* tell us who says what. Parentheticals convey attitude through the characters. Camera choices, visuals, props, and sounds are conveyed in upper case in description.

> JANE
> (flat, cool)
> Can we afford it?
>
> INCLUDE a beat-up Toyota, circa 1970s with a FOR SALE sign in the window, as Joe waves a PAYCHECK in the air and CLICKS his heels.
>
> JOE
> You betcha!
> Joe lands on the pavement with a THUD.

Effectively using technical elements to tell a story is a matter of developing your own technical style by trial and error. It begins with reading professional scripts to see how the tone and style vary according to technical choices that the screenwriter makes to create the emotional impact of the story. The secret is to know that the elements of screenwriting serve the elements of story, not the other way around. Paul Argentini's book *Elements Of Screenwriting*, the leading source book on this subject, will clarify questions you may have pertaining to technical style.

Confusing substance and form

Confusing substance and form is remarkably common, so constantly keep this distinction in mind as you move into creating the screenplay. The *elements of story* are the substance of the story, such as the story premise, dramatic situation, moral dilemma, dramatic complication, moment of insight, climax, and resolution. The *elements of screenplay form,* as originally defined by Syd Field, include the premise, first act plot point, mid-point, and second act plot point, climax, and the ending. The elements of screenwriting are the technical script requirements that you see on the page that convey the screenplay story.

Don't let the simplicity of this chapter fool you. Take it to heart, and you will be pleasantly surprised what it yields, both in the immediate future and over the years.

PART FOUR

Rewriting and Script Doctoring

"What is my story really about?"

CHAPTER TWENTY-TWO

Writing Is Rewriting

WRITING is rewriting. Storytelling is the talent of rewriting until you discover the subtle nuances within the story and know how to reveal them to add greater depth to the story. Once you have finished the rough draft of a script, the best thing to do is to leave it alone for a while, so that when you come back to it you can evaluate the project as if approaching it for the first time. As you look over the script in a relaxed mode, you will begin to define and discover script problems in a new way. Many writers share feedback with one another, which gives you some realistic sense of where you are in the process. Another route is to work with a script consultant or script coach who can quickly and easily identify the strengths and weaknesses of your story.

A script consultant or script coach helps you focus on solutions. Check out www.breakingin.net to find one.

As hard as it may be to hear criticism of your work, this feedback can prove invaluable to refining your screenplay. Try to keep an open mind all the while remaining aware of the source of your feedback. You may get (what seem to be) conflicting comments, and it's your job to remain open to the possibilities because one seemingly minor issue may need further examination from several angles before it can be integrated into the story or dismissed. The important thing to keep in mind is that all comments that you choose to integrate into your rewrite must make story sense! You will find that most comments, even those from non-professionals, convey something that can help your work, but they must be understood and interpreted in the context of the motives, abilities, and insights of the person making the comment.

REWRITING

Rewriting is a general term that refers to the development period of a script after the first draft or the original screenplay, including the period after the script has been sold and is "in development" with a studio or network. There are many stages in the rewriting process. In fact, the "Rewrite Phase" can take years for some projects because it's about rethinking the underlying elements of story, and questioning each and every element to see that you have asked the major storytelling questions. Even if you don't have all the answers, you are on the fast track to discovering where you want to take the story and how to get there. Above all, rewriting is not just about reworking scenes and revising dialogue; it's about solving story problems.

- **The Rewrite** The rewrite is the first rewrite of your original screenplay. The rewrite usually includes some story refinement and structural changes in the script, two sets of revisions, and a final go-round, called the polish.

- **The Rewrite-for-Hire** This is a draft where a second writer is hired to rewrite the original writer. This means the basic story idea is working, but the execution isn't there yet. The rewrite-for-hire also involves one draft, two sets of revisions, and a polish.

- **The Page-One Rewrite** This is a rewrite-for-hire where the concept is marketable, but the story is not working. The page-one-rewrite is very demanding, and often results in a completely different script from the original.

THREE STEPS OF REWRITING

Step one: rethinking spine

The most significant element of rewriting is rethinking your spine. If you accept the abstract nature of this wonderful process, you will free yourself to approach your story from an entirely new angle, even if you think you have already explored everything your story has to offer.

After assimilating comments from readers, I recommend giving your script a thoughtful read to see what's "on-story" and what's "off-story." This task will help you to see where the central conflict is developed, where it gets lost in scenewriting, and how to bring it back "on-story."

When I go through the process myself, more often than not, I find that characters have not been developed enough to benefit the story. By forcing myself to rethink the story through its spine, I usually come up with one or two ways to develop a new thread of the story that features the *opposing dramatic elements of the story through characterization.* Interestingly, discovering what is lacking within the antagonistic elements of story also reveals more nuances and greater depth of the main character. Sometimes this requires substantive structural changes; other times, it's just a matter of developing characterizations with greater accent, contrast, and poignancy within scenes that already exist.

Once new opportunities are identified, I recommend working through ideas and characters that create more conflict in the story, especially those that negate the spine. You may discover that your original spine is not strong enough to carry the entire story. If this is the case, rethinking the spine in entirely new terms is mandatory. In fact, this is the crux of the rewrite! In story terms, this requires redefining the central dramatic argument through the moral dilemma. Once you are on track, you can begin to experiment with characters, old and new, to strengthen the central dramatic argument or series of dramatic arguments that support and negate the new spine.

Developing the depth of the story through characters that portray dramatic argumentation is the essence of rewriting. It begins with eliminating haphazard characters and storylines, which neither reveal nor add anything to the story, and it becomes a process of developing characters that contribute to the thematic dramatic argumentation of the story. This is the "art" of screenwriting.

Step two: rethinking point of view

You may think you have already made the point-of-view decision in the first draft, but the reality is that this decision sometimes requires reader feedback in order to make the best choice for the story. In fact, you will be amused by the way readers immediately identify the point-of-view character that promises to keep your story on track. In fact, they often confirm their opinion by casting the point-of-view character for you! Invariably, they choose high profile actors (Anthony Hopkins, Meryl Streep, Ed Harris, Angelina Jolie) to make their point. What they are telling you is that they want their favorite A-list actor to tell your story.

....

Readers often cast the point-of-view character!

....

Listen carefully to all their suggestions, keeping in mind that people don't always say what they mean, but they always mean what they say. The audience needs continual understanding about the inner struggle of the main character, and this task is ongoing. It is accomplished by establishing an on-screen character who—*through conflict with the main character*—gives the audience insight into the story, from the beginning to the end. In other words, the character with the most conflict with the main character—both internal and external—is the best possible point-of-view character. However, point of view is established within the story by first defining the moral dilemma of the main character, and then establishing moral opposition to this dilemma through the point-of-view character. This dialectic—union of opposites—creates the on-going state-of-mind for the audience.

> Point of view = the union of opposites of the moral dilemma.

Step three: applying solutions

Applying your newly developed ideas, solutions, and characters begins with the task of looking at the major elements of your screenplay with a new perspective:

- ✓ **Where does the story begin?** This is the opening story point where the premise, or introduction of the story, is revealed through the main character. It is crucial to keep in mind that this opening story point may remain the same, but the scene itself is always under construction, being defined, refined, and redefined. This place—where the story begins—is the "set-up," which "pays off" at the climax of the story.

- ✓ **Integrating the newly developed spine into the twelve story sequences** This process begins with breaking down the events of the story, deciding what is "on-story" and what is "off-story," and then integrating the newly developed spine within the newly developed characters and threads of the story.

- ✓ **Building toward the climax with set pieces** Again, knowing where the story begins and how the logical story progresses toward its climax are essential, even prior to the first draft. Your new understanding of the climax reveals what the story is about in a deeper way, and now it's time to streamline the elements of the story to pick up momentum. In today's market, this means *streamlining your story points and evaluating your set pieces,* throwing out those that interfere with the momentum and fall flat, and developing those that offer dramatic pivots that push the story forward.

✓ **Shaping and developing scenes** This process is one of the most satisfying screenwriting tasks. After the story points are in logical story order, the deeper meaning of the story can shine through from scene to scene. Now that you finally understand, with greater depth, what the story is really about, you can work within scenes *to create the most conflict,* adding and subtracting characters to put more heat on each scene, creating poignant scene climaxes that push the story forward.

✓ **Staging the scenes** Staging is knowing when and how *to get into a scene* and when and how *to get out of a scene.* Although staging is usually the work of directors, it is important to know what the scene is about in story terms so you know how "to get in and get out" of the scene as a writer to advance the story for the reader. Study directors like Steven Spielberg, Ridley Scott, Andrew Davis, and Robert S. Butler for superior staging techniques. If possible, integrate film-editing skills into your repertoire so you can give your screenplay the feel of a professional storyteller.

✓ **What's the opening?** The opening is the first glimpse, or prelude, into the story. *It establishes the visual that conveys the tone, theme, and mind-set of the piece.* Like an overture to a stage musical, it's the "Once upon a time . . ." moment when the audience signs onto the story. After you have committed to the major rewrite decisions, you can begin brainstorming about the opening. This is such a crucial decision—for marketing as well as storytelling—the director often holds off making the decision until production or post-production. In any case, delaying this decision is the norm, so it's the writer's job to present more than one alternative to the director.

✓ **What's the ending?** When the essential rewrite elements are finally in place and the story logic and story structure are well defined, the ending flows at breakneck speed. Like the opening, don't be afraid to experiment with several endings—audiences love surprise endings—and don't be afraid to take the final set piece to the limit!

✓ **The revised "one-page"** When the rewrite is complete, the spine gradually becomes clear. Not only are you ready to rewrite the one-page featuring both the inner struggle of the main character and the external story, you should be ready to transpose your movie into a powerful visual concept.

Rewriting the Rewrite

Once the rewrite is thematically and structurally sound, the project enters the preproduction phase. At this juncture, the objective is to attract a star and a director so the new rewrites are specific to what the script needs:

The Character Rewrite The character rewrite has a specific goal and purpose. Once your story is clear, the character-driven structure will emerge through the main character, and the character rewrite serves to attract a major movie star. The process involves rethinking the emotional story so you can create the "inner story" with greater clarity, featuring the progression of moral choices of the main character, such that the audience engages with the transformation of the main character by action and unconscious identification. The character rewrite is the advanced rewrite, which can be broken down into eight steps:

1. Redefining the moral of the story Begin by seriously thinking about the moral of the story and whether it is clearly realized from the premise of the story as the main character's moral strength is tested. This means going back to each *story beat* to make sure the main character's internal conflicts are on-story.

2. Developing internal and external conflicts Return to the premise, and as you evaluate the story beats, go back through each scene and rethink the internal, unconscious conflict to assess whether the emotional story progresses dramatically through the external conflicts of the events of the story. Without a doubt, there will be room for improvement, usually in the overall momentum, scene by scene, and conflict by conflict. Refining specific threads of the subplots scene by scene as they feed into the story, and character by character as they support and negate the spine, also builds to the climax.

3. Main character solutions In storytelling, most solutions are created through characterization. Usually the main character can be more fully developed through specific behavior and deeds that reflect the inner story. The task here is to differentiate between problem-solving by depicting deeds and behavior of the main character vs. tapping into supporting characters to develop the main character's internal story.

4. Supporting character solutions Inevitably, there are two or three supporting characters that you may not have developed to your best advantage. This is the time—before your script goes to market—to clarify what you need in order to convey the emotional story. This requires redefining supporting characters, determining which characters can and should be further developed, or which should be eliminated. This sophisticated task will elevate your script to a new level that is immensely satisfying.

5. The three-beat rule All subplots pertaining to supporting characters have their own three-beat plots within the story. In other words, once you decide which supporting characters tell the story of the main character, then you can work with each supporting character's subplot thread and make sure each character has his own three-beat "story" or "character arc" with a beginning, middle, and end.

6. **Visual solutions: images and actions** Sometimes visual solutions, such as images or simple actions by the main character, suffice. Always consider visual possibilities *in comparison with* problem-solving by creating a scene with supporting characters. If a simple image or action by the main character works, then so be it, but if you can possibly open up the story to a more sophisticated level through internal conflict revealed by external conflict with a supporting character, then take the time to think it through—not just in one scene or moment, but by using the relevant supporting characters and subplot threads from beginning to end.

7. **Dialogue solutions** Many screenwriters are tempted to problem-solve with dialogue. This can be marvelous if you write like Tennessee Williams or Jason Miller. For the vast majority, however, defining the unconscious drives of your main character is difficult, you might begin by recording "dialogue solutions." This will give you the discipline to evaluate different ways to translate story fragments or dialogue into meaningful visual images, character action, or conflict with supporting characters.

8. **Eliminating extraneous characters and dialogue** This is your last chance to get rid of characters who may mean something to you, but have no bearing on the story. Extraneous characters and subplots can derail your screenplay.

The Comedy Punch-Up

The punch-up refers to a comedy rewrite, as in sharpening the comedic punch lines and cutting those that fall flat. The punch-up also involves improving the rising action of the scenes, intensifying scene climaxes, and building sequence climaxes, all of which help to create a more effective story climax.

Especially in comedy, if any scene of your screenplay does not build toward the story climax, it's crucial to evaluate what elements of the scene, if any, might be folded into another scene. Extraneous moments and scenes interfere with the progression of story beats and prevent your discovery of how to use them to reveal another layer to your story. From a practical perspective, don't put yourself in a position where irrelevant scene moments make it to the editing room. Not only is it difficult to recover continuity and pacing in post-production, sometimes it's too late to cut these moments without losing story sense. Comedy has some exceptions in this regard, but the principle also applies to drama as well.

Sight gags Audiences love visuals. Just the sight of Eugene Levy wearing dreadlocks in *Bringing Down the House* as an expression of his love and devotion for Queen Latifah sent audiences reeling with laughter. Also, who can forget the apple pie "love scene" in *American Pie*?

Running gags Again, Eugene Levy's infatuation with Queen Latifah in *Bringing Down the House* began with romantic desire for her sassy way, developed into "wigga rap" love poems, and climaxed with his willingness to surrender his white-a** lawyer life for his sexy lady love. Notice how the progression of "rap gags" repeat and develop, building a romance with a beginning, middle, and end.

The three-beat comedy rule Three is funny. Most jokes, gags, and dialogue are structured in threes. Even subplots are structured in threes, as in *Tootsie*: 1) Dr. Brewster makes a pass at Julie (Jessica Lange), and Dorothy (Dustin Hoffman) admonishes him. 2) Dr. Brewster makes a pass at Dorothy, and she slaps him, demanding to be treated like a person. 3) Dr. Brewster serenades Dorothy, and Dorothy is forced to invite him in to shut him up.

The 180° reversal In *Tootsie*, there are 180° reversals—character reversals—throughout: Michael (Dustin Hoffman) is three hours late for his date with Sandy (Teri Garr). She confronts him with the fact that she saw a woman (Dorothy) enter Michael's apartment, but ends up falling for Michael's lame excuses, criticizing Emily Kimberly's performance (actually Michael's) for not being tough enough. Rather than admit to his own mistreatment of women, Michael begins rewriting Emily's lines, and stands up to the obnoxious French-kissing Dr. Brewster with a cattle prod to zap his patooties.

Politically incorrect In general, American audiences love to hear the iconoclastic truth about what is really going on behind closed doors in the political arena, as opposed to what political pundits declare as politically correct. In movies, however, especially in wartime when lives are at stake, audiences tend to favor traditional themes that support the troops. Box office hits that feature traditional political themes include *Air Force One, Clear and Present Danger,* and *Black Hawk Down.*

Literal contrast One of the most successful devices in comedy is to introduce an intellectually challenged character who only understands literal thinking. *Dumb and Dumber* made a fortune based on two characters who carried the entire movie with literal thinking. Adding one literal character with running gags provides brilliant contrast for the straight-man or straight-woman main character.

Paradox The main character claims to be a certain stereotype in the heroic mode, and at the same time, does the exact opposite. Steve Martin provokes nonstop laughter as he struggles to be a great filmmaker in *Bowfinger,* but succumbs to mediocrity by breaking all the rules.

Irony The main character denies being a certain stereotype and then proves his denial false by contradictory behavior. Jim Carrey in *Liar, Liar,* proves his denials false from beginning to end.

Hyperbole The main character agrees with his or her worst critics and proves it by exaggerated behavior that amuses us. Robin Williams in *Mrs. Doubtfire* proves he is willing to go to any lengths to redeem himself with his children.

The Polish-for-Hire

This is the last draft in the development stage of the script, prior to the green light for production. The purpose of the final polish is to eliminate extraneous description, unnecessary shots, superfluous action, and expository dialogue. More important, the polish brings each scene into focus by sharpening dialogue and scene climaxes, and opens up the last frontier of voice, tone, symbolism, and unconscious meaning.

Extraneous description Eliminating superfluous scene description is word-by-word warfare. It is the writer's responsibility to take out every word that interferes with the images and action of the characters.

Unnecessary shots Often, a story requires fewer shots than the writer imagines. The simple presentation is always preferable, especially for submission to a studio.

Superfluous action Each scene has an overall action by the main character, and an overall action that opposes the main character. Actions and conflict that do not advance the story will eventually be deleted, and it's best to remove them yourself at this stage.

Expository dialogue Even if you do your best to guard against it, expository dialogue finds itself onto the page. The key is to find it before others do, and transpose it into actable conflict, visuals, or action that advance the story.

Sharpening dialogue Some people have a genius-level ability with conflict and dialogue, but cannot structure a character-driven story or a screenplay. Others can work through story problems, create a magnificent character-driven structure, but are tone deaf. Generally speaking, dialogue is considered a lower-level talent than creating the story and character-driven structure of the screenplay. However, as you cross the finish line of a well-structured screenplay, brilliant dialogue becomes essential to the marketability of your script to a movie star, so it's worth the struggle to evaluate each and every line of dialogue. Keep in mind that dialogue can be improved at any time: on the set, or even in post-production, so it's never too late to come up with more pithy or touching lines, even for minor characters.

Unconscious meaning Keep in mind that the audience infers more from your story than you intend, so don't hesitate to deliver unconscious interpretations and meanings during the final polish. The best final touches eliminate obsolete dialogue in favor of action and visuals to portray unconscious meaning.

The Director's Movie

Once you have sold your script, your project literally and legally belongs to a production company for the duration of the option, or in perpetuity when the option is exercised and the purchase price is paid. Your script will hopefully attract an A-list director and star, and get a green light or go-ahead from the studio. Now, what was once your screenplay becomes the director's movie and you enter the script doctoring phase.

SCRIPT DOCTORING

Although rewriting and script doctoring may sound similar, they are, in fact, quite different. Rewriting refers to script development before production. Script doctoring refers to *rewriting the script for production* under the supervision of the film director when the project has received a "green light" or "go-ahead" from the studio or network to begin production. Usually there are stars attached at this point, so the project has a definite direction and production date, with a strong leader who has specific time deadlines.

Top writers such as Stephen Zaillian (*Searching for Bobby Fisher, Schindler's List*) often work directly with a top director from page one, tackling script problems associated with production from the onset. It's not unusual for a writer of this stature to require more than one year, and sometimes two, to complete a screenplay for a major studio, even in association with a major director.

Working with the director can be good or not so good. It is good if the director wants to keep you on board during the pre-production and production phases. It is not so good if the director has a different vision and wants to personally rewrite the script or has a preferred writer for this purpose. In any case, the movie is no longer yours, and the proof is that the director's name will probably be listed above the title in what is called a *possessory credit*.

Vision: The Director's Concept

If the director has an entirely new concept in mind, or a different vision from yours, the script's green light may be subject to major script doctoring revisions. Some movies have a very interesting history in this regard:

The Godfather, prior to Francis Ford Coppola's involvement, was a novel and screenplay by Mario Puzo. When Robert Evans, then president of Paramount Pictures, approached Coppola to direct the project, Coppola turned Evans down because he wanted to tell the story of America through an Italian family, as opposed to a traditional mobster melodrama. After repeated rejections on both parts, both Evans and Coppola finally agreed to the new vision—Coppola's! Thanks to the script doctoring phase, *The Godfather* became one of America's best-loved epics, earning Mario Puzo and Francis Ford Coppola the Academy Award for Best Screenplay Adaptation.

Tootsie, originally written by Murray Shisgal, also has an interesting rewriting history. The script had been through writer after writer, with a total of eleven rewriters. It wasn't until Academy Award–winning director Sydney Pollack came on board to work with the enormously talented Larry Gelbart, that they were able to discover the spine of the story, and shape the entire script, for which Shisgal and Gelbart won the Academy Award for Best Original Screenplay.

The Production Rewrite

The director assembles his or her production team and the set writer works with the team to adjust the script to production, taking into account physical limitations and cost overages. The set writer supports the practical demands of the movie-making process, which, at this stage, is more task-oriented than creative. The main objective is to clarify dialogue for the actors and specify production requirements for the director of photography, assistant directors, production manager, production designer, set designer, property master, make-up and hair stylists, stuntmen, and director of special effects. Last, but not least, the editor, who puts the movie together shot by shot in the editing room, needs to be kept apprised of production rewrites.

The Dialogue Polish Some directors believe in rehearsal, others do not. There is always room for improvement with dialogue, so the set writer accompanies the production during rehearsal in case dialogue changes need to be made on the set, which they inevitably do. Sometimes directors bring back the original writer to recapture the "voice" of the main character, which may have been diluted through all the rewrites.

The Final Shooting Draft Even when the script seems to be written in stone, there is still plenty of room for improvement on the set, from shot to shot. Once the production wraps, all the changes are recorded into what is now called the final shooting *draft*.

Post-Production Rewrites Rewrites keep on coming in post-production, even after the movie is completely assembled by the film editor. Lines are written, rewritten, and looped or dubbed to improve the on-screen performances until the picture is "locked" into its final film edit, after which sound effects, sound mixing, and the musical score are added.

The Legal Draft

After the sound effects are added and music is scored, a transcriber records the final text. This is known as the legal draft, which becomes the finished version of the script, the basis for the copyrighted version of the picture.

The Release Print

The copyright symbol © is internationally recognized, but a little-known fact is that a copy of the release print of the movie is sent to the Library of Congress at 4:30 P.M. the afternoon before the picture opens. It arrives the next morning, just before theater doors open to moviegoers all across America. Given the enormity of this process from beginning to end, no wonder it takes a team of lawyers to protect the copyright of the release print, owned by the studio that releases the movie, backed up by United States' and international copyright laws.

Final Note About Rewriting

Although the primary challenge of creating an A-list screenplay is to create a compelling role for a major movie star, the overriding talent is the ability to approach the process of writing and rewriting with an open mind. Moreover, it is impossible to achieve a multi-layered screenplay without old-fashioned discipline, drive, and perseverance. As you labor alone at the keyboard, keep in mind that many, if not most, A-list screenplays find their niche in the marketplace—after several rewrites. Sometimes it can take two years to find the A-list element, sometimes a decade. Rewriting is the key to *creating an A-list screenplay that sells!*

PART FIVE

Breaking In and Staying There

CHAPTER TWENTY-THREE

Breaking In

BREAKING in is such a popular subject among screenwriters that I was recently asked to chair a panel, "Breaking In and Staying In," at the UCLA Extension Writers' Program Writer's Faire, which takes place in early September every year at the UCLA–Westwood campus. This event attracts hundreds of writers and student-writers from all over Southern California, including the graduate departments at Loyola Marymount University, California Institute of the Arts, University of Southern California, California State at Northridge, and others. Our 2003 "Breaking In" panel included producer-manager Frederick Levy and writer-producer Ron Wilkerson, and our lively discussion attracted an overflowing crowd.

Ironically, it requires almost as much originality to get a job in the entertainment field as it does to create an original screenplay. In fact, we all have such interesting stories about breaking in that we still share them with one another in professional forums and at social events, long after we have crossed that difficult threshold. In fact, breaking-in stories have been elevated to an art form among professionals, part folklore and part apocryphal. And what makes the art form so entertaining is that everybody has a unique story!

COMMON SENSE

Before offering some up-to-date tips for getting a professional job as a screenwriter, here are some common-sense suggestions to keep in mind as you head into the marketplace with a completed script:

- It is considered bad form to talk about your writing in social situations until the script is completed and registered at the Writers Guild of America. Ideas have a short life span, and if your idea is passed along from a friend to a friend to a friend—even innocently—it can be misappropriated by someone else who casually heard it on the tennis court or the golf course, but has no idea where it originated.

- Conversely, keep in mind that at any given time, there are several scripts being written on similar subjects, and sometimes the exact same subject. This is why you must register everything—treatments, step outlines, and scripts—with the Writers Guild of America (www.wga.org), which verifies the legal date of registration. Then, when it's time to sell your material, it should be marketed through a licensed literary agent, preferably one that is franchised by the Writers Guild of America. Guild franchised agents carry extra prestige in the entertainment industry because they abide by the customs, rules, and regulations pertaining to U.S. Copyright Law and the Basic Minimum Agreement of the Writers Guild of America, as well as guild agreements pertaining to the Directors Guild and Screen Actors Guild. Credibility is everything when it comes to getting your screenplay read by production companies, and it's worth the wait to get a literary agent who is widely respected and lends credibility to your work. If you have any questions about whether your prospective agent is franchised by the WGA, contact the agency department.

• As a courtesy to fellow writers, it is also recommended that you not discuss what your friends are writing unless it is already sold, in which case, there is usually a publicity announcement surrounding the sale that draws attention to the topic so that other buyers and sellers do not imitate or lift the subject matter.

FINDING AN AGENT: CERTIFICATE OF AUTHORSHIP

When you buy a house, the escrow and title companies that handles the transaction for both the buyer and the seller requests title insurance to investigate the title of the house to make certain that the seller is, in fact, the true owner of the property, and has the legal right to sell the property. This is to insure the buyer against any and all parties who may lay prior claim of ownership to the property after the transaction closes. When you sell a movie, a similar process exists. The buyer (producing entity) requests a *certificate of authorship* through your literary agent, which states that you, as author, are the sole author of the property they are purchasing, and by signing this certificate you agree to indemnify the buyer against any and all claims of plagiarism that could arise pursuant to this statement. This is the first step of what is known as the *chain of title*, and there will be other steps as the script develops and financial partners participate in the movie financing. Literary agents keep this uppermost in mind when they consider representing material. There are four essential questions you will be asked.

1. *Who are you?* While this does not require fingerprinting and an FBI investigation, it does raise questions regarding your background and ethics. Some agents have been burned so badly that they require a lawyer or manager to vouch for you and the origin of your material before they will consider returning your telephone call or responding to your letter of inquiry. Others will consider a new client only if highly recommended by a current client who has personal knowledge of you and pertinent information regarding the origin of your material. In any case, there is no getting around this

issue of *who you are,* and this includes your personal reputation and character.

2. *How did the project originate?* The question here pertains to whether you are its sole author; whether anyone (as producer, director, or otherwise) helped you in developing the story and script; whether there are underlying rights such as published material, prior written material such as a treatment, play, or book; and whether there are life rights of a true story involved. There is no getting around this vetting process, because eventually the buyer will ask you the same questions. In fact, the buyer will expect you to answer a series of questions and make a written statement, which indemnifies them from plagiarism, alleged or otherwise. If you deceive the agent or buyer about these fundamental issues, eventually you will be found out. Not only will your career be short-lived, your movie will not get made because no insurance carrier will insure it for errors and omissions. If you temporarily succeed, but are later contradicted by another writer, producer, or director who worked with you or person whose true-life story you have exploited, you will learn that U.S. copyright laws and their legal precedents are very strict. You will also learn that agency laws are strictly applied, as are the Writers Guild of America rules and regulations. Disclose everything pertaining to the origin of your literary property to your potential agent.

3. *Where has the project been?* Keep in mind that the literary agent's career is based on personal reputation and credibility. This is someone who is licensed by the state where he or she practices, and franchised by the Writers Guild of America. This is someone who is entrusted with other people's money and who makes a living by knowing copyright law, agency law, as well as the customs, rules, and regulations pertaining to the Writers Guild of America. When a WGA franchised agent rejects you or your work for any reason that involves the copyright or an ethical breach pertaining to copyright, it is up to everyone involved (especially you!) to pay attention to the

reason(s). This means that every subsequent literary agent you may contact to represent you or your material will want to know these details. In fact, if there is any question whatsoever pertaining to copyright, the new agent will want to know everything about the origin of the project, *not from your perspective*, rather *from the perspective of the agent who questions the origin of the material due to existing copyrighted material or another contributor to the project.*

4. *How do you conduct yourself with buyers?* While it may appear that anything goes in the entertainment field, there is actually a great deal of protocol involved, both stated and unstated. The ability to take creative instruction is a given, but also at issue is the writer's ability to take legal instruction from an agent or lawyer when, and if, a contractual conflict occurs. Even casual customs reflect the buyer-seller relationship. How meetings are set (and cancelled) is a sophisticated process meant to safeguard time. It's not personal. Respecting boundaries is essential, and recognizing that these buyer-seller relationships go back many years is essential. This is a marketplace-driven business about making movies that make money. Turn off your cell phone during a meeting. Do not disturb people at home, at night, or during their weekends to blather on about your new idea or how you plan to sell your screenplay. Learn to organize, contain, and present your thoughts at a time when the listener, especially the buyer, is apt to listen. Don't be fooled by false appearances that suggest "Attitude is okay, and manners are passé." If the producer's wife, the director's assistant, or the movie star's girlfriend is offended by your behavior, take a hint, tone it down, and brush up on a few things your parents taught you. This used to be called behaving like a lady or a gentleman; whatever it's called today, it hasn't gone out of style.

BREAKING IN

Most people break into the entertainment field in a capacity other than writing, and then make the move into screenwriting while they are making a living in the business and getting to know the buyers and sellers from inside. There are a few screenwriters who get hired directly based on a great script—and knowing just the right person—but there is a drawback to this get-famous-quick strategy. Without the benefit of a number of long-term relationships, it's very difficult to sustain a long-term career in the entertainment field. That being said, here are some of the most direct, practical tips that have proven to be the best ways to break into the film business as a screenwriter:

Win a Screenwriting Contest

This is the most direct way to gain entrée into the film business as a screenwriter. There are hundreds of contests, but your objective is to impress an agent or buyer, so it is important to be selective. According to *Screenwriter Magazine Online* (www.nyscreenwriter.com), there are forty-six (forty-six!) screenwriting contests that are widely recognized among film professionals. (For a list of competitions, see Appendix B.) Keep in mind that placing in the semifinals of a major competition is a major accomplishment, while placing as a top ten finalist of the Motion Picture Academy's Nicholl Fellowships in Screenwriting (www.oscars. org/nicholl) carries so much prestige that it virtually guarantees that you will find an agent. My friend and associate David Cowper took my class at UCLA twice, won first place in UCLA's Diane Thomas Screenwriting Competition, then became a finalist in the Academy's Nicholl Fellowship; the next thing you know, he sold his first script!

www.breakingin.net

Check out www.breakingin.net on the World Wide Web for the very latest information on screenwriting competitions, information about what's happening in the industry, professional standards and format, copyright law, letters of inquiry, protocol pertaining to meetings, and how to network through legitimate industry sources and professional organizations. You will find just about everything you need to know about getting your foot in the door, plus links to many other pertinent websites. (For a list of important websites, see Appendix C.)

The Mailroom

Historically, the William Morris mailroom was the place to begin a career in show business. Presently, this translates to working in the mailroom at any of the big packaging agencies, such as William Morris Agency, Creative Artists Agency, International Creative Management, Paradigm, and Metropolitan Agency. Packaging agencies are large talent agencies that package movies by attaching bankable stars and directors to literary material before they are submitted to a studio. By contrast, literary agencies represent and sell literary material directly to production companies who package the movie after the script or material is sold. David Geffen and Barry Diller started in the mailroom and climbed their way to the top!

The Entertainment "Temp Agency"

Skip the mailroom. Learn how to type scripts as you learn how to write scripts, get a temp job at a studio, get your foot in the door, and move up the ladder. This is an exciting way to get to know the industry from the inside at a higher level of entry. With a bird's-eye-view of how the marketplace works, you can rule out the jobs you don't want to do, figure out where the opportunities are, and strategize how you can succeed.

Script Reading

While you are looking for that big break as a writer, hone your craft by studying the mistakes of others as a professional script reader. This is one of the most popular routes for writers, but with a serious drawback. You work alone, rather than networking in the marketplace, getting to know the buyers and sellers on a daily basis. It's a good first job, but you need to be in the swim of things to advance. Sherry Lansing, Lydia Woodward, and Dana Stevens started as readers, and never looked back!

Script Research

Attach yourself to a great screenwriter as a researcher. This is usually accomplished by becoming an assistant or reader first, and then becoming known among writers and producers as reliable and thorough in your approach to script. In my own case, I made headway in my own career by working with Tennessee Williams, and then moving forward with other (A-list) writers such as John Sacret Young, William Hanley, Reginald Rose, Tom Rickman, T. S. Cook, and Frank Pierson. Not only did I learn a tremendous amount from these gentlemen, their personal guidance set me on a career path known for quality entertainment.

Journalism

The AP desk or UPI desk are one of the best ways to platform yourself into a career in show business. Because journalists are perennially in pursuit of the story, they bring a sophisticated approach to the process of storytelling. Also, journalists and media feed the studio publicity pipeline, so journalists enjoy a special entrée into show business. Some of the most interesting screenwriters come from a journalism background: Charles MacArthur & Ben Hecht (*The Front Page*), Kurt Luedtke (*Absence Of Malice*), Frank Swertlow (*Babies*), John Riley (*For Ladies Only*), and Joe Eszterhas (*Basic Instinct*).

Acting

This list of actors-turned-screenwriters speaks for itself: Sylvester Stallone, Steve Martin, Billy Crystal, Carrie Fisher, Ben Affleck, Matt Damon, Jason Miller, and Carl Gottlieb.

Production

Working production, regardless of how menial the position, is a great way to get a feel for the film business. You will get a chance to roll up your sleeves, put yourself to practical use, and observe how the script evolves during pre-production through production.

Teachers and Nurses

During production, there is always a nurse on the set. If there are minors in the cast, there is also a schoolteacher. If you can afford the flexibility, this is an excellent way for teachers and nurses to break into the business. Without giving up your day job, you can develop access to talent, producers, and directors.

Post-Production

Post-production involves film editing, sound editing, and music editing. This fascinating avenue introduces you to script mistakes that might have been avoided during the screenwriting process. How directors and producers bring a story into focus after the filming is completed is an eye-opening experience. Some directors of the highest stature began their careers in the editing room, including Sir David Lean, Andrew Davis, and Graeme Clifford.

Internships

College internships are a great way to get your foot in the door. Loyal alumni have an interest in promoting their own, and after graduation, you already know people who are in a position to offer you a job. The Writers Guild of America (www.wga.org) offers a mentor program. The Directors Guild of America (www.dga.org) sponsors internships. Warner Bros. Comedy and Drama Writers Workshops (www.warnerbros.com/writersworkshops) are well known for the success rates of their participating writers, and The Walt Disney Studios and ABC Entertainment

Writing Fellowship Program (www.abctalentdevelopment.com) is so well respected, even professional writers apply for the opportunity.

Uncle Syd or Aunt Mary

There is nothing quite like family when it comes to breaking into show business. They know you best, and are usually willing to go to bat for you, especially when it comes to asking a literary agent to read material. Having an aunt, uncle, or cousin in the business is great, so is a friend of a friend. With respect to personal connections, keep in mind that the friendly assist stops with the introduction. Once you get your foot in the door, the rest is up to you.

Breaking into show business is about creating an opportunity. Staying in show business is about preparation, hard work, and self-promotion. One without the others is worthless. Those who are offered opportunities before they are ready often regret not being better prepared. Those who break in by hard work sometimes wish they had discovered the art of self-promotion. The self-promoters invariably wish they knew more about script, especially when their first movie flops. Everyone must learn the same lessons, but in a different order.

CHAPTER TWENTY-FOUR

Second Careers and Reinventing Yourself

ALTHOUGH the film business appears to be dominated by young writers, the reality is that it usually takes several years to learn how to write a screenplay, and several screenplays to learn how to write a *great* screenplay. With maturity, a deeper understanding of life emerges inside all of us. Screenwriting is such an attractive second career because our youthful preconceptions lose their harshness as we move toward a greater appreciation of humanity, and the storytelling process opens up creative possibilities of expression. Veteran screenwriters who have sustained a career over several decades understand this principle better than anyone. They recognize that it's one screenplay at a time, with levels of personal growth in between.

The key to longevity for a veteran screenwriter is the same for a beginning writer as it is for a second-career screenwriter. It's about discovering your unique voice and creating an original screenplay with a strategy to market your unique talent on a new level. We call this *reinventing yourself.*

The beauty of reinventing yourself is that *anybody* can reinvent him- or herself with an original screenplay, manuscript, or newly published book—regardless of age, gender, background, or experience. The challenge is to create something big enough to appeal to the mainstream audience and feature your unique talent with a long-term career strategy that helps you ride the waves of the marketplace, which seems to favor young writers, unsuccessful sequels, and movies based on video games and comic books, over original screenplays by mature storytellers.

SECOND-CAREER SCREENWRITERS

The vast majority of my students and clients are second-career screenwriters, ranging in age from twenty-five to seventy-five. Virtually all of them are well educated and highly accomplished, many at the top of their fields. They are attracted to storytelling because they have a unique life experience that motivates them and have a compelling story to tell. My roster has included doctors, lawyers, college professors, a female FBI agent, a former CIA operative, an LAPD weapons expert, an internationally known economist, a top divorce lawyer, a top cinematographer, an MTV director, a famous songwriter, psychologists, nurses, teachers, real estate agents, novelists, publicists, journalists, playwrights, film editors, ad executives, documentarians, film animators, criminal defense attorneys, engineers, rocket scientists, and techies. One of the most unusual screenwriters I have worked with is a nuclear physicist who took the summer off from Harvard University to learn screenwriting with me through UCLA Extension Writers Program. The interesting by-product of working with so many talented second-career screenwriters is the degree of mutual respect that arises among colleagues.

REINVENTED SCREENWRITERS

Virtually all screenwriters who are writing an original screenplay are reinventing themselves. Those who enroll in a formal class are acutely aware of the goals and objectives they wish to achieve. Several have already sold screenplays, and then find themselves unable to make headway with a particular subject matter. Others have succeeded at writing television half-hour comedy or starred in television series or movies and want to learn character-driven story structure in screenplay form. Others have mastered the mini-series genre, but want to learn more about visual storytelling for the big screen. Even the most accomplished screenwriters in the film business reinvent themselves from time to time. It's never too late.

The Objective vs. the Goal

The objective of reinventing yourself is specific. At the very minimum, the purpose is to establish yourself with a project that makes a splash in the marketplace. This is called an A-list submission. It means your story or script is so original—so unique—that the Hollywood A-list hears about it through the grapevine or at industry events and *calls your agent to get a copy.* Your agent is suddenly besieged with telephone calls from the producers and executives who run the studios and companies for major players such as Steven Spielberg, Tom Cruise, Tom Hanks, Julia Roberts, Sydney Pollack, or Barry Levinson. Your agent sets the distribution date for the screenplay submission, and the A-list companies send their own messengers to your agent's office to pick up your script!

The goal is also specific. Your agent wants to create a bidding war, or *auction,* surrounding your script or manuscript, so you merit a substantial six-figure (or possibly seven-figure!) deal with an A-list company. Even if your script does not sell, you have successfully reinvented yourself at the A-list level, and based on the quality of your work, may be hired to do a script-for-hire, rewrite, or adaptation by executives or producers at an A-list company.

Think big. Be prepared. And go for it!

Agents readily admit that lightning usually strikes once in a screen-writer's career with a big sale, and the trick is to have a treasure trove of material ready to sell when it strikes, as well as enough writing experience to make the most of any scripts-for-hire, rewrites, and adaptations that come your way. This may require years of preparation, but hopefully, the reward will be worth it.

Taking a meeting

The art of taking a meeting is misunderstood. It involves a performance where you become an actor and a writer, learning how to listen to cues, understanding what is said, and interpreting what is really being said and what is expected of you. Taking a meeting is filled with subtlety and nuance. Knowing how to socialize in a business setting is essential, but the time of the buyer is limited, and it's a capital crime is to waste your meeting on a story that is not worked out or does not appeal to the buyer. The best sales meetings are short: You have something to sell that they want to buy. The best rewrite meetings are long: They believe you can solve the script problems that are presented one at a time. If you have trouble taking a meeting your career will fizzle, so don't be afraid to learn this art form under the guidance of an experienced producer or manager who sends you friendly cues, especially the exit cue. The best source book on this subject is *How to Write It! How to Sell It!*, written by UCLA Senior Instructor Linda Palmer, who has been both a studio executive and producer.

Doing lunch

The art of doing lunch is Public Relations 101. It's about being seen with your agent when your script is on the market. It's about being seen with producers when your script is not on the market. It's about being seen with stars and directors whenever possible. It's about being seen! However, the secret here is that it's also about not being heard! Let others do the talking. Fill them in on past work, give them a little preview of what you are up to, but don't give your stories away over lunch. Let your agent recommend when and where you pitch full-length stories. Withhold a little; no freebies, not even to your best friend, the producer!

STRATEGIES FOR MOVING TO THE A-LIST

Discover your voice

We each have a unique voice, but discovering and integrating that voice into storytelling is another matter. By *voice* we mean a one-of-a-kind worldview. If you think of this as your personal mind-set, a window that opens to the world of ideas, you are on the right track. When your voice is fully developed, it's similar to DNA. When people hear yours, they not only know it's you, they also know it cannot possibly be anyone else.

Become an expert

This is the quickest route, especially for those transitioning into screenwriting as a second career. One of my friends, Paula Thrasher, has a very interesting autobiographical story, which she adapted into a novel, based on her experiences as the top female diamond expert in the world. Not only did she rise to the top in the male-dominated world of the diamond trade, eventually she was invited to become a sightholder on the Belgian Diamond Bourse, which is closely held by Hassidic Jews. As the first woman, first gentile to enter this exclusive world, Paula was able to parlay her professional expertise into a work of fiction, *The Sightholder's Promise,* which her film agent, Bernie Weintraub, of Paradigm Agency sold for screenplay development.

Specialize in a genre

Pick your genre. James Cameron picked science fiction, which gave him the credibility to do his signature epic, *Titanic*. David Webb Peoples picked Western, *Unforgiven,* which won him the Academy Award. Cameron Crowe picked character-driven pieces and made a name for himself with major stars. Other A-list specialists include: Shane Black, action; Joe Eszterhas, thriller; James Carabatsos, war movies; M. Night Shyamalan, supernatural thriller; Steven Zaillian, biographical epic. Take your pick. Write something original. But remember, you are in competition with the best of the best.

Develop public speaking skills

Believe it or not, appearing in public matters. If you want to become a celebrity writer, then you might as well get used to the spotlight. Beware, however, that those who live by the sword, die by the sword. Too much public speaking may take away from your writing and dilute your ability to develop your unique voice.

Be seen

Like taking a meeting and doing lunch, this is great advice because it is so simple. When your script goes to market, make it a point to be seen wherever you can. Most agents want to create an aura about you as your new script is slipped to the A-list, so another cagey way to attract attention to yourself is to be seen hobnobbing at the best lunch places. Remaining a mystery can work in an exclusive submission, but this is a hyped-up world, and being seen anywhere and everywhere by the A-list when your script is on the market is an excellent strategy.

Publish a book

Although easier said than done, the publishing world is closely aligned to the film business. Examples of recent major motion pictures with powerful stories, based on previously published material include: *Lord of the Rings: The Return of the King, Seabiscuit, American Splendor, Mystic River,* and *Cold Mountain.* Some of the greatest movies ever made are adaptations: *Schindler's List, The Godfather, The Wizard of Oz, One Flew Over the Cuckoo's Nest,* and *Gone With the Wind.*

Use the media

Movies are about marketing. Anytime you can use the media to promote your movie, your script, a book related to your movie, or the star of your movie, you are reinventing yourself as a writer and promoting your movie as a viable commodity in the film business. Some writers even hire a publicist for this purpose. The key is to target the various windows of opportunity *at the right time.* Recognize the best moment to promote yourself, then shift to the best moment to promote your script so you can attract a star, and finally, know when and how to promote the movie through movie stars when it opens. How much is too much? Don't worry, you'll know. The media junket stops—when the next hot movie opens!

Reinventing yourself presupposes you already have established yourself in a certain arena and have something to offer. It does not mean letting go of your integrity; it means opening up your world and talent to other avenues of expression that lead you to discovering your unique voice.

Becoming a Storyteller

IS it the journey or the destination that intrigues us as storytellers? Sometimes the journey seems overwhelming, but once the destination is on the horizon, the journey becomes the destination. As one of my screenwriting colleagues at UCLA, writer-director Chris Canaan, so sardonically states, "Most people say they want to write a screenplay, but what they really mean is that they want to 'have written' a screenplay."

Don't be surprised, if after finishing a screenplay, you may feel you want to plant a garden, play basketball, go fishing, go shopping, play golf, or take a little vacation. You may even swear you never want to write another word, let alone another screenplay, as long as you live! Then, suddenly, something will strike your fancy, an idea that can become a big idea—a new project that sparks your enthusiasm like a red-hot flame! Weary of rewrites and suffering from carpal tunnel syndrome, you find yourself resisting the urge to write, and are ready to throw in the towel, but something keeps drawing you back to that new big idea. It begins percolating involuntarily overnight, and then it starts taking over your mind during the day. A short time later, you wake up one morning and you understand what story you want to tell, what genre you want to tell it in, with specific characters and ideas that reveal something very personal you have experienced about the subject matter. And presto! It's no longer a matter of creating the project—the project is creating itself *as a story* because you have successfully crossed the threshold of *becoming a storyteller*!

When the final product speaks for itself with a screenplay sale or rewrite-for-hire, you cannot believe your good fortune, but more importantly, you can hardly believe how much you have developed internally as a person by discovering the many hidden truths within your material. Not surprisingly, some of the most profound discoveries we make about life become our stories, and conversely, some of the most complex realizations we discover as storytellers become the basis for our deepest convictions as human beings.

It is the unity of the *journey and the destination* that define us as human beings. One without the other is lacking. How we live our lives is as important as the goals we achieve. As we are living our lives to their fullest potential as creative, thoughtful human beings, hopefully we are learning the capacity to respect one another and the ability to enjoy the journey along the way with affection and admiration for one another. And if you are lucky enough to be professionally recognized by your peers with an Emmy, a Peabody, a Christopher, or an Oscar, you may experience the surprise question from friends who admiringly ask, "What does it feel like?" You may only imagine your response today, but I guarantee that what may look like glamour and glory actually *feels like work*, deeply personal work from within your heart and soul.

So, go forth screenwriters, work from inside your heart and soul. And remember this amusing anecdote as the final secret to becoming a storyteller:

The late Sir David Lean, one of the most respected and honored filmmakers in the history of film, was known to be a perfectionist about everything he did, especially *Lawrence of Arabia*. In fact, he was so dedicated to the quality of his work that he re-edited the film twenty-five years later for its twenty-fifth anniversary re-release with Columbia

Pictures, and he couldn't resist adding one more tweak day-in and day-out, adjusting the dialogue, the final edit, the final dub, even the musical editing. He communicated his never-ending list of detailed changes to the editor every morning, noon, and night. As the re-release date drew near, the never-ending list of subtleties and nuances continued, *and this was twenty-five years after he won the Academy Award!* Finally, the editor had to lock him out of the editing room. No doubt, Sir David tried to pick the lock.

Now, that's a storyteller!

APPENDIX A

Entertainment Industry Organizations

Academy of Motion Picture Arts and
 Sciences
8949 Wilshire Blvd.
Beverly Hills, California 90211
(310) 247-3000
www.oscar.com

Academy of Television
 Arts and Sciences
5220 Lankershim Blvd.
North Hollywood, California 91601
(818) 754-2800
www.emmys.tv

American Cinematheque
Lloyd E. Rigler Theatre at the Egyptian
6712 Hollywood Blvd.
Hollywood, California 90027
(323) 461-2020
www.americancinematheque.com

American Film Institute
2021 North Western Ave.
Hollywood, California 90027
(323) 856-7600
www.afionline.com

Directors Guild of America
7920 Sunset Blvd.

Los Angeles, California 90046
(310) 289-2000
www.dga.org

Los Angeles County Museum of Art
Leo S. Bing Theatre
5905 Wilshire Blvd.
Los Angeles, California 90036
(323) 857-6000
www.lacma.org

Producers Guild of America
6363 Sunset Blvd., 9th Floor
Los Angeles, California 90028
(323) 960-2590
www.producersguild.org

Screen Actors Guild
5757 Wilshire Blvd.
Los Angeles, California 90036
(323) 954-1600
www.sag.org

UCLA Film and Television Archive
James Bridges Theatre
1409 Melnitz Hall
UCLA Campus, Westwood 90024
(310) 206-8013
www.cinema.ucla.edu

Writers Guild of America
7000 West 3rd Street
Los Angeles, California 90048
(323) 951-4000
www.wga.org

Screenwriting Competitions

There are hundreds of screenwriting competitions, but some are not widely recognized by agents, managers, and producers. Others gobble up your entry fee without offering anything in return to advance your career. Here is a list of the top twenty screenwriting competitions based on industry recognition:

TOP TWENTY SCREENWRITING COMPETITIONS

Nicholl Fellowships in Screenwriting
www.oscars.org/nicholl

Sundance Institute Screenwriters Lab
www.sundance.org

Alfred P. Sloan Fellowship (Science and Technology) with Sundance Institute
www.sloan.org

Warner Bros. Comedy Writers Workshop
www.warnerbros.com/writersworkshop

Warner Bros. Drama Writers Workshop
www.warnerbros.com/writersworkshop

The Walt Disney Studio and ABC Entertainment Writing Fellowship Program
www.abctalentdevelopment.com

The Humanitas Prize
www.humanitasprize.org

American Film Institute/Maui Writers Conference Screenwriting Competition
www.afionline.org

American Zoetrope Screenplay Contest
www.zoetrope.com

Nickelodeon Productions Fellowship Program
www.nick.com/allnick/fellowshipprogram

International Family Film Festival Screenplay Competition
www.iffilmfest.org

Tribeca/Sloan Film Program
www.tribecafilminstitute.org

Independent Feature Project
   IFP/Chicago Production Fund
   IFP/LA Screenwriters Lab
   IFP Market – Emerging Narrative Section
   IFP Screenwriting Award
www.ifp.org

Klasky Csupo Writing Competition
www.klaskycsupo.com

Chesterfield Film Company Writer's Film Project
www.chesterfield-co.com

New York Foundation for the Arts Artists' Fellowship
www.nyfa.org

Monterey County Film Commission Screenplay Competition
www.filmmonterey.org

Variety "Pitch Me" Competition
www.variety.com/pitchme

Breckenridge Festival of Film Screenplay Competition
www.breakfilmfest.com

NICHE AND REGIONAL SCREENWRITING COMPETITIONS

There are many other important screenwriting competitions for niche filmmakers or up-and-coming writers from specific regions. Check out nyscreenwriters.com, moviebytes.com, scriptsales.com, and breakingin.net for the latest information about opportunities that may be tailored just for you:

American Cinema Foundation Screenwriting Competition
Asian American International Film Festival Screenplay Competition
Austin Film Festival Prime Time Television Competition
Austin Heart of Film Screenplay Competition
Cinequest San Jose Film Festival Screenplay Competition
Cinestory Screenwriting Awards
Cynosure Screenwriting Awards
Film in Arizona Screenwriting Competition
Gordon Parks Independent Film Awards
Mania Fest Screenplay Competition
McKnight Artist Fellowship for Screenwriters
Nantucket Film Festival Screenplay Competition
Nevada Film Office Screenwriting Competition
New York International Latino Film Festival Screenwriting Contest
Organization of Black Screenwriters Screenwriting Contest
Project Greenlight (HBO—Live Planet)
Rhode Island International Film Festival Screenplay Competition
Set in Philadelphia Screenwriting Competition
Slamdance Screenplay Competition
SLAM FI Sci Fi Screenplay Competition
Washington State Screenplay Competition

APPENDIX C

Popular Internet Websites for Screenwriters

www.asascreenwriters.com: The American Screenwriters Association

www.atomfilms.com: Atom Films: Short Films

www.breakingin.net: Everything you need to know about breaking in!

www.celluloidjungle.com: Celluloid Jungle: general screenwriting source

www.creativescreenwriting.com: *Screenwriter* magazine

www.dga.org: Directors Guild of America

www.empire-pov.com: *Point of View* magazine

www.fadeinmag.org: *Fade In* magazine

www.filmfilm.com: Independent Film Financing Sources

www.finaldraft.com: Final Draft: contests, research, software

www.harvestmoon.com: Harvest Moon: legitimate shooting scripts

www.hcdonline.com: *Hollywood Creative Directory*

www.hollywood.com: Hollywood: hot news!

www.hollywoodnet.com: The Hollywood Network (for screenwriters)

www.hollywoodreporter.com: *The Hollywood Reporter*

www.ifilmpro.com: Who's Who in Hollywood

www.ifp.org: The Independent Features Project

www.imdb.com: Internet Movie Database—for box office and film credits

www.inzide.com: Zide/Perry Management—accepts submissions

www.iscriptdb.com: Internet Script Database—find professional scripts

www.mandy.com: Mandy: jobs!

www.moviebytes.com: Movie Bytes: excellent contest information and general source

www.netflix.com: Net Flix: DVD rentals

www.nyscreenwriters.com: *New York Screenwriter*—great!

www.screenplayers.net: Screenplayers: post your bio & script

www.screenwriter.com: Screenwriter: online classes

www.screenwritersroom.com: Screenwriters Room: advice from film executives

www.screenwritersutopia.com: Screenwriters Utopia: networking

www.scriptcrawler.com: Script Crawler—find professional scripts

www.scriptimp.com: Script IMP: from your script to the producer's ear!

www.script-o-rama.com: Drew's Script-o-rama: find professional scripts

www.scriptsales.com: Script Sales: recent sales

www.scriptshark.com: Script Shark: move your script up the food chain!

www.scriptteaser.com: Script Teaser: subscribers are screened

www.scriptwritersnetwork.com: The Writers Script Network: general source

www.simplyscripts.com: Simply Scripts: find professional scripts

www.storybay.com: Storybay: access to agents and producers

www.studioscriptsales.com: Studio Script Sales: staff of agents and producers

www.sydfield.com: Syd Field: the one and only!

www.thewritersjourney.com: Christopher Vogler & *The Writer's Journey*

www.ucla.unex.edu: UCLA Extension Writers Program: #1 for screenwriting

www.variety.com: *Variety*

www.wga.org: The Writers Guild of America—Mentor Program

www.whorepresents.com: Who Represents: how to find the star for your movie

www.wordplayer.com: Ted Elliot and
Terry Rossio—everybody loves
them!

www.writersdigest.com: *Writers Digest*

www.writersscriptnetwork.com:
Writers Script Network: promote
your screenplay

www.writerswebsite.com: Writers
Website: post your loglines for free

www.zoetrope.com: Francis Ford
Coppola's e-zine

APPENDIX D

"Standard U.S. Format" and Elements of Screenwriting

"Standard U.S. Format" is approximately 100 to 120 pages, on 8½" x 11" three-hole paper, typed in 12 pt. Courier, bound with three brass fasteners with cardstock covers.

RECOMMENDED SOURCES

Argentini, Paul. *Elements of Style for Screenwriters*.
   Hollywood, California: Lone Eagle Publishing Company, 1998.

Lerch, Jennifer. *500 Ways to Beat the Hollywood Reader*.
   New York: Fireside/Simon & Schuster, 1999.

Spec Format Guide
   Fade In magazine

Final Draft
   This is the leading software program for Elements of Screenwriting and Format. Go to www.finaldraft.com

Screenwriter
   This is another formatting program that also lets you view your scripts in outline (card) form. Go to www.screenplay.com

All sources are available through The Writers Store at www.writersstore.com

Bibliography and Recommended Reading

BOOKS

Field, Syd. *Screenplay: The Foundations of Screenwriting (Third Edition)*.
New York: Dell Publishing, 1979, 1982, 1994.

Franklin, Jon. *Writing for Story*.
New York: Plume, 1986.

Hegel, Georg. *Phenomenology of Spirit (Phenomenologie des Geistes)*
Germany: 1806.

Hegel, Georg. *Science of Logic (Wissenshaft der Logik)*
Germany: 1812–1816.

Hunter, Lew. *Lew Hunter's Screenwriting 434*.
Chapter Four: The Outline for You and "Them"
New York: The Berkley Publishing Group, 1994.

Mamet, David. *On Directing Film*.
New York: Penguin Books, 1991.

McKee, Robert. *Story*.
New York: Regan Books, 1997.

Seger, Linda. *Making a Good Script Great (2nd Edition)*.
Hollywood, California: Samuel French Trade, 1987, 1994.

Vogler, Christopher. *The Writer's Journey: Mythic Structure for Writers. (2nd Edition)* Studio City, California: Michael Wiese Productions, 1998.

VIDEO RESOURCES AND UNIVERSITY-RELATED LECTURES

Costa, Joseph P., Esquire. *Legal Instruction: Copyright Law & Certificate of Authorship*.
Excerpts from legal instruction pertaining to Copyright Law & Certificate of

Authorship by copyright expert Mr. Joseph P. Costa, Esquire. Summarized in a lecture prepared by Kate Wright for UCLA Extension Course "Writing the Screenplay the Professional Way."

Gehred-O'Connell, Mark. *Science Fiction Genres.*
Excerpts from hand-outs for UCLA Extension Online Course "Writing Science Fiction for Television and Film."

Lipton, James. *Inside the Actor's Studio: Sydney Pollack.*
New York: New York University Film School
Arts & Entertainment Network, copyright, 1995.

Mason, Dr. Albert. A. *Character Development.*
Excerpts from lecture about characterization by USC Professor of Clinical Psychiatry Dr. Albert Mason. Summarized in hand-outs prepared by Kate Wright for UCLA Extension Course "Script Doctoring: Rewriting for Production."

ELECTRONIC RESOURCES

Butler, Clark W., Ph.D. Chapter Eight, *Negation of the Negation.*
www.ipfw.edu/phil/faculty/Butler/Chapter8Negationof theNegation.PDF

Ludwig Feurbach and the End of Classical German Philosophy: *Part 1: Hegel.*
"Frederick Engels, Ludwig Feurbach and the End of Classical German Philosophy." Germany: 1886.
http:www.marxist.org/archive/marx/works/1886/ludwig-feurbach/ch01.htm

TVGuide Online: *Movie Database.*
TV Guide Magazine Group, Inc., 2003.
Available from *Cinebooks Database.*
http:www.tvguide.com/movies/database

Wright, Lenore. *"Genre Supports Structure—But Doesn't Replace It!"*
Break into Screenwriting: Movie Genres, Screenplay Structure.
http:breakingin.net/genrestructure.htm

Wright, Lenore. *Dream Jobs to Go! Screenwriter: How to Break into the Screenwriting Business.*
DreamJobsToGo ebook, 2001.
http:www.dreamjobs.com

INDEX

About the Author

Emmy Award–winning writer-producer Kate Wright is currently writing and producing *Billy*, a major motion picture based on biographer Diane Wood Middlebrook's book *Suits Me: A Life of Billy Tipton*, featuring the true story of enigmatic jazz musician Billy Tipton, who upon his death was discovered to have been a woman who lived her life as a man for over fifty years. Wright also recently completed *The Conspirator Saint*, an independently funded epic feature film screenplay based on the life of St. Katharine Drexel of Philadelphia, who was canonized in October 2000 in Vatican City.

Ms. Wright, Senior Instructor of Screenwriting at UCLA Extension's internationally known Writers Program since 1995, teaches "Writing the Screenplay the Professional Way" and "Script Doctoring: Rewriting for Production." Having worked with major talents such as Pulitzer Prize–winning playwright Jason Miller and the legendary Tennessee Williams, she also works as a script consultant. In addition to studio screenwriters, her client list includes novelists, playwrights, doctors, lawyers, a former CIA operative, an FBI agent, an LAPD weapons expert, first-time screenwriters, as well as feature film directors and producers. *Screenwriting Is Storytelling* (Perigee Books, 2004) is her first book.

Ms. Wright, who received an Emmy for The Magical World of Disney's *A Mother's Courage: The Mary Thomas Story* starring Alfre Woodard, has also been honored with the Christopher Award, Wilbur Award, Youth in Film Award, and American Women in Radio and Television Award. She and Producer-NBA Hall of Famer Chet "the jet" Walker have also received the NAACP Black Image Honor for positive portrayal of African-American role models in *A Mother's Courage: The Mary Thomas Story* as well as *The Father Clements Story*. From 1982–1990, Wright served as Vice President of Interscope Communications, producer of numerous motion pictures and television movies, including *Three Men and a Baby*, *Outrageous Fortune*, *Cocktail*, and *The Hand That Rocks the Cradle*. As one of

Interscope's founding members, she acquired books, scripts, and true stories for feature films and television: *The Father Clements Story, American Geisha, Stillwatch, The Jessica McClure Story, The Secret Life of Archie's Wife,* and *Cocktail,* starring Tom Cruise, which grossed over $300 million worldwide.

Ms. Wright, a member of the Independent Feature Project West, the International Documentary Association, and the Academy of Television Arts & Sciences, resides in Los Angeles. She is a licensed real estate agent in the State of California and affiliated with Coldwell Banker's Beverly Hills office, the #1 residential real estate office in the world. She participates in numerous civic and charity events, especially for Georgetown University, for whom she co-wrote and produced *Georgetown Then and Now,* Georgetown University's Bicentennial Celebration, hosted by Disney Chairman Michael D. Eisner, and televised live from Constitution Hall in Washington, D.C., to forty-seven cities. She participates in live media events for UCLA Extension Writers Program, UCLA's Writers Faire, Georgetown University's Entertainment Symposium, and Sherwood Oaks Experimental College; and she is often featured on popular internet websites such as www.breakingin.net and www.screenwriter.com.

Prior to her career in entertainment, Ms. Wright worked in the U.S. House of Representatives and the U.S. Senate, after earning degrees from the Georgetown University School of Foreign Service in Washington, D.C., and the Sorbonne University in Paris, France. Her pastimes include cooking, reading, entertaining, architecture, opera, and golf.